SCOTLAND

Jack Altman

JPMGUIDES

Contents

Fàilte gu Steòrnabhagh
STORNOWAY

This Way Scotland

The attractions of its rugged landscape, the elegant cities and rustic villages, not to mention the people, are powerful enough to let you forget the weather. No one is likely to go there for a suntan, but Scotland will invariably bring a healthy glow to the cheeks of any visitor with an ounce of curiosity or affection for natural beauty, the monuments of a strong and ancient tradition and the fiery, independent spirit of the Scots themselves.

Cultural Identity

Scotland has a cultural identity as distinctive in flavour as its whisky. Just as the most popular brands subtly blend fine single malts with rougher grain whisky, so Scotland happily integrates the essence of its legendary charms with the sometimes harsher realities of everyday life. Of course, Scotland is more than its tartans, haggis, bagpipes, golf courses, castles shrouded in the mists of the glens—and, yes, the whisky, too. Beneath these colourful frills, the people themselves have a new serious sense of purpose born of the ever stronger aspiration to social, economic and political autonomy within, and beyond, the United Kingdom.

The Mainland

Scotland is bounded by the Atlantic Ocean to the west and north, the North Sea to the east, and England to the south. A channel of barely 22 km (13 miles) separates the Kintyre peninsula from Northern Ireland. With its 78,750 sq km (30,400 sq miles), Scotland covers over a third of Britain's total land surface, but its 5 million inhabitants make up only a twelfth of the national population. A crow flying from the mainland's northern tip at Cape Wrath down to the southernmost point of Galloway would cover 450 km (280 miles). At its widest point, the mainland is some 250 km (155 miles) across, but its river estuaries (firths) and deeply indented coastline make the sea rarely more than 70 km (43 miles) away.

The Borders, or Southern Uplands, stretching from the boundary with England to Glasgow and the capital Edinburgh, offer lush green pastures for sheep grazing in the rolling hills and rich farmland of the Tweed Valley. The region was the home of writers Robbie Burns and Sir Walter Scott.

The Central Lowlands are low but not at all flat, the hills rising

3

Just the place to get away from it all—a lonely house in the Highlands, on the shores of Loch Duich.

quickly to the castle country of mountains, steep-sloped glens (valleys), forests and the lochs of the Trossachs. Over on the east coast are fishing villages, seaside resorts and the university town of St Andrews (also well known to the golfing community). On the west coast, Argyll's spectacular scenery includes some beautiful subtropical gardens and a wilder Atlantic coastline.

The Northeast extends from the industrial cities of Dundee and Aberdeen across the whisky country to the Grampian Mountains. The Grampians boast Britain's highest peak, Ben Nevis, 1,343 m (4,406 ft).

The Highlands come into their own beyond the fault line traced by the Great Glen, northeast from Fort William along its elongated lochs—notably Loch Ness—over to Inverness. Ice Age glaciers eroded the Highland plateau, resulting in mountain peaks and deep glens. The three coastlines have quite distinct personalities: green meadows and woodland in the east; wild and windswept in the north; tranquil sandy coves alternating with rocky headlands in the west.

The wildlife includes red deer, foxes, badgers and otters—with grey seals, porpoises and dolphins in the Atlantic and North

Sea. While hunters are on the lookout for red grouse and pheasant, birdwatchers are happy to spot golden eagles, osprey, buzzards, peregrine falcons and a host of gannets, guillemots and other seabirds along the shores.

The Islands

Scotland's islands are divided into three main groups. Buffeted by the Atlantic Ocean, the principal islands of the Western Isles (formerly the Outer Hebrides) are Lewis and Harris, barren and rugged but blessed with fine sandy beaches. Closer to the mainland are the 12 islands of the Inner Hebrides, including the Isle of Skye with its dramatic scenery and grand Cuillin hills, Mull, Iona and Islay. The third group, the Orkney and Shetland islands north of the mainland approaching the Arctic Circle, are a world apart, both from Scotland and from each other, often more Scandinavian than Scottish in landscape and temperament.

The People

Encounters with warm-hearted, hospitable and generous Scots make any visitor wonder where on earth they got the reputation for being miserly. As with any people anywhere, the poorest of them may be of necessity frugal, but certainly not mean. With the reinforced national pride of recent years, English is often spoken with a more pronounced Scottish accent than before. Scots, a form of Anglo-Saxon best recorded in the poetry of Robbie Burns, is the dialect of the south and northeast. Gaelic (a Celtic language brought over from Ireland and pronounced "Gallic") is making a strong comeback in the Hebrides and western Highlands, as well as in Glasgow.

The Cities

Home of the new parliament, the capital Edinburgh has always been the dignified champion of the Scottish national identity with its theatres, fine arts museums and university.

Glasgow, Scotland's biggest city, was for long almost written off as a grimy industrial monstrosity. But since the 1990s it has bounced back with renewed vigour as a major cultural centre. It boasts splendidly restored 19th-century and Art Nouveau architecture, vibrant art galleries, theatre, opera and concert halls—and some of the wittiest repartee in Europe.

On the northeast coast, the granite city of Aberdeen thrives in a thoroughly modern manner from its North Sea oil riches or, as its people say, putting Aberdeen's money where Edinburgh's mouth is.

5

Flashback

In the Beginning...

...was a rock. Edinburgh's Castle Rock makes a good vantage point from which to imagine much of Scotland's story from its geological beginnings to its parliamentary present. The city's heights were created by volcanic upheavals 70 million years ago. During the Ice Age, glaciers eroded the softer stone to leave high and dry the hard black basalt core of the Rock on which the royal castle was to be built. Down below, around 7000 BC, Stone Age Celtic hunters and fishermen made their way west along the Firth of Forth. By about 1500 BC, settlers had started farming. From 850 BC, the tribes were fending off marauders from the safety of hill forts such as the Rock. In the 1st century AD, the Votadini Celts looked over the wooden parapets of their earthworks at Roman legions marching to subdue bellicose tribes further north. Just east of the Rock on a ridge formed by volcanic debris, the future monuments of the Royal Mile would be built between the Castle and Holyrood Park, home of a medieval abbey, the 16th-century royal palace—and today, the site of the new Scottish Parliament building.

Scotland's First Peoples

When Julius Caesar invaded Britain in 55 BC, he did not continue up to Scotland, and it was not until AD 80 that the first Roman troops under Agricola pushed north across the Tweed Valley to the Forth. Three years later, at the battle of Mons Graupius (in the Grampian Mountains), Agricola's army crushed the Caledonian tribe which provided the Roman name for Scotland. Agricola's son-in-law, the historian Tacitus, described the Romans' looting, killing and raping and added: "Wherever they make a wilderness, they call it peace" *(ubi solitudinem faciunt, pacem appelant)*.

In fact, Agricola was recalled to Rome before he could complete the conquest of Scotland. His successors shored up, or rather walled up, the peace, first by building Hadrian's Wall from the Solway to the Tyne in the north of England (in 121), then, twenty years later, the Antonine Wall 160 km (100 miles) further north. This extended about 60 km (40 miles) from the Clyde River to the Firth of Forth, part of it running through Falkirk. Beyond it lived the Picts, who perhaps derived their name—*Picti* (painted) —from body tattoos. Apart from

The standing stones of Callanish were set up by the earliest inhabitants of the Hebrides.

a few desultory incursions, the Romans preferred to leave these unruly tribes of Celtic or pre-Celtic peoples to their own devices. Scotland shows no traces of Roman civilization comparable to the towns and villas of southern Britain.

After the Romans abandoned Britain in the 5th century, Scotland was divided among four distinct peoples. The Picts dominated the northeast and the northern Highlands. Anglo-Saxons spread up the southeast coast to occupy the Lothians up to the Forth. Britons moved into the southwest Strathclyde region. From Ireland, the Gaelic Scots (*Scotti* to the Romans) settled in the Western Isles and Argyll (*Argael* means "Eastern Irish").

Birth of a National Identity

It was the immigrant Irish who performed the major Christianizing role in the country, beginning the slow process of unifying the rival peoples and stamping the Scottish name on the nation that emerged. The chief missionary was the Abbot St Columba (521–597); he built a monastery on the isle of Iona as a base from which to bring the Celtic Church to the mainland. An earlier mission of St Ninian among the Britons of Strathclyde was taken up in the

7

6th century by St Kentigern, also known as Mungo, founder of the church in Glasgow. After initial conflicts, the ascetic and traditionalist Celtic Church submitted to Rome, but resisted unification with the Church in England.

Growing numbers of Scots settlers spread their religion and Gaelic language through the Pictish heartland, which was weakened by Norse raids in the 8th and 9th centuries. In 843, Kenneth MacAlpin, Scottish lord of Kintyre, was proclaimed king of both Picts and Scots in the church of Scone (just north of modern Perth), to which the sacred Stone of Destiny had been brought from Ireland. By the middle of the 11th century, MacAlpin's descendants had won control by marriage, war and dynastic infighting—most famously involving Macbeth—of practically all the land we now know as Scotland. Only the islands were excluded: from the 9th century onwards, Norsemen had settled Orkney, Shetland and the Western Isles (Hebrides) and confirmed their rule by treaty in 1098.

In securing the southern borderlands of Strathclyde and the Lothians, Macbeth's successors—Malcolm III and his sons Edgar, Alexander and David—brought about an influx of Anglo-Norman lords and a loose allegiance to the English king.

Under David I (1124–53), elements of the English feudal system introduced a semblance of order after the rough and ready

"FAIR IS FOUL AND FOUL IS FAIR"

Whatever some talented English propagandist may have claimed, Macbeth, king of the Scots from 1040 to 1057, was really not such a bad fellow. Unlike the English (in so many things), the Scots did not pick their kings by primogeniture and so Macbeth's claim to the throne of his uncle, Malcolm II, was at least as legitimate as that of Malcolm's grandson Duncan, who got there first. Macbeth killed Duncan in open battle near Elgin, not furtively in bed at Glamis. Though only two of the previous nine kings died a natural death, Macbeth felt secure enough on his throne to make a pilgrimage to Rome, where "he scattered money like seed to the poor." When Macbeth was in turn killed in battle by the future Malcolm III, it was, as Scottish patriots point out, only with the help of English soldiers. As for Lady Macbeth, much as Shakespeare enjoyed frightening his audiences, he decided not to overdo it by calling her by her real name: Gruoch.

governance of the Scots' fiercely independent Celtic clans. The Norman-educated king gave key Scottish lands to the Anglo-Norman aristocracy—Frasers, Bruces, Haigs and Stewarts. He also appointed Anglo-Normans to new Scottish bishoprics, among them Glasgow, Caithness and Aberdeen, and founded several monasteries. David ruled the country with English-style sheriffs, judges and administrators governing from royal castles which the king visited in rotation. He minted Scotland's first independent silver coinage and fostered trade in Edinburgh, Stirling and Berwick by conferring on them the relatively autonomous status of royal burghs. As the English language—and Norman French—spread north of the Forth into the Lowlands, Gaelic became the preserve of the Celtic Highlands.

Braveheart versus the Hammer

In the 140 years following David's death, the Scottish kings played a delicate balancing act with their rapacious English neighbours. One important success was Alexander III's acquisition of the Hebrides from the Norwegians in 1266. His death in 1286 left the throne up for grabs.

Six years later, Edward I of England was able to impose a compliant successor, John Balliol, who duly pledged allegiance to the English throne. When even the docile Balliol found Edward's demands too humiliating, he formed an alliance with the French and invaded the north of England in 1296. Edward earned his nickname of "Hammer of the Scots" by countering with a massive invasion that crushed all Scottish resistance. With the support of Scottish nobles such as Balliol's arch-rival Robert Bruce, the English destroyed Berwick, at the time the wealthiest city in Scotland, slaughtered Balliol's forces at Dunbar and seized Edinburgh, Stirling, Perth and Elgin. In the ultimate act of humiliation, Edward carried off the Scots' sacred Stone of Destiny from Scone and imprisoned Balliol in the Tower of London, leaving Scottish affairs to the Earl of Surrey as his viceroy.

The Earl preferred the comfort of his Yorkshire estates, even when Scottish rebellion erupted after the English sheriff of Lanark was killed in May 1297 by one of Scotland's great national heroes, William Wallace, who has latterly achieved fame once again in Mel Gibson's film, *Braveheart*. Born into a family of respectable but not noble landowners, Wallace was spurned by Scottish lords prudently paying allegiance to Edward. Wallace's fervent but 9 raggle-taggle army, vastly outnumbered by English forces, fought a brilliant—and brutal—guerrilla warfare of lightning raids from the depths of the forest of Selkirk. They avoided pitched battle until joining up with the northern troops of Andrew Murray. Their advance on Stirling on the River Forth forced the English viceroy to leave his Yorkshire haven to fight in Scotland. His army was trapped on Stirling Bridge when the Scots swooped down from the hills, killing 5,000 English infantrymen and 100 cavalry.

For his victory, Wallace was knighted and made Guardian of the Realm (on behalf of the imprisoned Balliol). His efforts to unite the country were thwarted by Scottish nobles including Robert Bruce. Edward returned from France to conquer Wallace's army at Falkirk in July 1298. Seven years later, Wallace was arrested, hanged, drawn and quartered. It was only then that Bruce turned against Edward and had himself crowned King Robert I of Scotland (1306–29). In 1314, he scored a devastating victory at Bannockburn, when the English lost 30,000 men. Six years later, with the Declaration of Arbroath, Robert won the Pope's support for Scottish independence, recognized by England in the Treaty of Northampton in 1328.

Squandered Independence

Independence from England did not mean unity. The monarchs of the Bruce dynasty, which died out in 1371, and the Stewarts who followed, many of them infants when they came to the throne, were unable to impose their authority on the fierce rivalries of Scottish lords acting as regents. The Douglas clan effectively controlled most of southern Scotland. The Macdonalds ruled in the northwest, Lords or, as they preferred, Kings of the (Western) Isles, siding with the English. Further north and east, the Highland lords were a law unto themselves. A judicious marriage of James III Stewart with the Scandinavian princess Margaret did bring in 1469, as part of her dowry, the islands of Orkney and Shetland.

In order to strengthen their hand against the English, the Stewarts exploited Scotland's "Auld Alliance" with France. In exchange, hoping to divert English energies being deployed against the French, James IV's troops invaded Northumbria in 1513. The disastrous battle of Flodden Field ended in the death of 10,000 Scots, including the king and the flower of his nobles and Highland chiefs. Henceforth, Scotland's independence from England was little more than nominal.

Mary Queen of Scots

James V's marriage to Marie, Duchesse de Guise made acutely apparent the perils of alliance with France. Instead of a counterweight to preserve Scottish independence from England, the alliance threatened to hand over Scotland lock, stock and barrel to the French. After James's death in 1542, Mary Queen of Scots succeeded her father to the throne when she was still in her cradle, not one week old. Her French mother resisted pressure from England's Henry VIII to marry Mary to his little son Edward. With the enraged Henry's armies storming through Scotland, Mary was bundled off to France. The French king exulted: "France and Scotland are now one country." Mary was brought up at court as a thoroughly French—and Catholic—lady and became François II's queen at 17. But however much they preferred the French to the English, the menace of being absorbed by France rather than England was not quite what the Scots wanted.

In 1561, upon the death of her husband, Mary returned to occupy her Scottish throne. On the Tudor side of her family, she was also a claimant to Elizabeth's English crown and faced a power struggle between pro-English and pro-French factions. This in turn was aggravated by the Reformation conflict between her Catholic supporters and Protestant adversaries. The sermons against idolatry of John Knox, fiery leader of the Scottish Reform church, or "Kirk", resulted in widespread destruction of statues and paintings in monasteries and Catholic churches. After Knox met with Mary to warn against "ungodly" behaviour, her wish to hear Mass at her chapel in Edinburgh caused rioting at Holyrood Palace.

Matters were not improved when Mary married her arrogant Catholic cousin, Lord Darnley, who was intent on becoming king rather than mere consort. He had Mary's Italian secretary and overly influential favourite, David Riccio, murdered at Holyrood and was himself strangled soon after. Mary then married the man widely regarded as responsible, the Earl of Bothwell. The fact that Bothwell was a Protestant did nothing to placate the scandalized Scottish clergy and nobility, Protestant and Catholic alike. Forced to abdicate in favour of her baby son James VI in 1567, Mary fled to England a year later. Elizabeth imprisoned this legitimate rival to the English throne until she had her executed in 1587.

Civil War and the Restoration

With strong English support, James VI (1567–1625) was raised as a Protestant who opposed the Scottish drift towards a strict Calvinistic Presbyterianism independent of royal authority. In 1592 the Presbyterians managed to replace the rule of royally appointed bishops with a Synod and Presbytery operating as legal church courts for both ecclesiastical affairs and public morality. After Elizabeth's death in 1603, the Scottish king also became James I of England, but he was obliged to keep the two thrones separate. However, he was strong enough to bring back Scottish bishops. From 1610, they acted in association with the Kirk's synods and presbyteries, but the stage was set for future religious strife under James's uncompromising successor.

Charles I (1625–49) was born in Scotland but English-bred, with a taste for the pomp and ceremony of the High Anglican Church and no sympathy for the austere Scottish Reformists. His attempt to impose Anglican-style prayers and liturgy in 1637 provoked the formation of a National Covenant to resist, among other impositions, the "Popery" of these alien forms of worship. In anger, Charles called a General Assembly of the Kirk, which responded by abolishing his Scottish episcopacy. He then tried military force, but after humiliating defeat by the Scots' well-equipped troops in the Bishops'

Wars (1639–40), he could not persuade a hostile English Parliament to finance a stronger army. Instead, by 1642, the king found himself with a Civil War on his hands.

The Covenanters governed Scotland till 1651 and gave their support to the English Parliamentarians. In 1646, Scottish forces captured Charles at Newark in Nottinghamshire and handed the unrepentant monarch over to the English rebels. Most Scots, however, condemned the king's execution in 1649 and were ready to side with his son, Charles II. Oliver Cromwell headed the English army that defeated Scottish royalists at Dunbar in 1650 and Worcester a year later. Under Cromwell's army of occupation, an imposed parliamentary union governed fairly and efficiently until the Restoration of Charles II as king of both England and Scotland in 1660.

Charles II was very much an absentee landlord, not once visiting Scotland in the 25 years of his reign, preferring to rule by decree from London. He brought back the bishops, but this time they worked with the synods and presbyteries and did not try to impose Anglican practices. The general tolerance of Charles's rule won acceptance from all but the most recalcitrant old Covenanters. They were defeated by English

Much accomplished and full of charm, Mary Stewart led a life of adventure and intrigue, but was too dangerous for the English queen Elizabeth.

forces at Bothwell Bridge in 1679, but pockets of often bloody resistance continued over the next decade. Things were worsened by Charles's successor, his brother James VII of Scotland and James II of England (1685–88). An out and out Catholic, James made support for the Covenanters a capital crime of treason. His policy of giving high office only to Catholics appeared, even to moderate Scotsmen, to threaten the very existence of their Presbyterian church.

Union with England

After England's "Glorious Revolution" of 1688 to oust the Catholics (and their French backers), James was forced to flee to France and yield the throne to his Protestant daughter Mary and her Dutch husband William of Orange. Dutch William, as the Scots called him, showed no interest in their country beyond letting them preserve their Presbyterian church, abolish Anglican bishops and effectively end their religious wars.

It was Mary's sister Queen Anne (1702–14) who oversaw the Act of Union of 1707 to ensure Protestant succession and fend off the threat of re-conquest by James II and his Jacobite followers in Highland Scotland. The 13

English gained Scotland's support by dangling the economic benefits of free trade while buying off key leaders with dukedoms and other material inducements. With guarantees for their separate legal system and Presbyterian Kirk, the Scots voted to merge their parliament into one British Parliament based in London—with 45 Scottish commoners and 16 lords.

Fearing the Catholic Stewarts more than they disliked the English Protestant Hanoverians, most Scots were hostile to Jacobite uprisings in favour of James II's Stewart successors. Thirty years after an abortive rebellion in 1715, Charles Edward Stewart, "Bonnie Prince Charlie", led a triumphant force of Highlanders through Scotland and over the English border down to Derby. The uprising, known as the Forty-Five, collapsed for lack of promised French support. Bonnie Prince Charlie was driven back to the Highlands where his troops were slaughtered at Culloden, near Inverness, in 1746. He fled to the Continent and died 40 years later in drunken disillusion.

Defeat was followed by repressive measures that included a ban on tartans, bagpipes—"an instrument of war"—and the bearing of arms. The break-up of the Highland chiefs' private armies put an end to their clan system. No longer militarily useful, their tenants now proved to be an economic burden. Sheep farming on the highland pastures replaced less profitable cattle and crop farming.

Modern Times

By the early 19th century, the peasants were being forcibly moved off the land in the notorious Highland Clearances. The tenants saw their homes burned to the ground as they were obliged to emigrate to North America, England or the southern Scottish cities, while the Lairds used the estates for the entertainment of profitable hunting, shooting and fishing parties from the south. A few remaining peasants eked out a living as crofters on small patches of barely arable land.

The picture was radically different in southeast and northeast Scotland where progressive agriculture and cattle farming helped to feed Scotland's rapidly growing population. Despite the Highlanders' emigration, the population of the country rose in the 19th century from 1,500,000 to 4,500,000. This was due to improved medical care, mass immigration from Ireland during the potato famine of the 1840s, and a certain prosperity from large-scale industrialization—notably Glasgow's textiles and Clydeside shipbuilding, Falkirk iron and the coal mines of southern Scotland.

World War I cost Scotland 74,000 lives but also proved a boon to Clydeside shipbuilding, engineering and munitions manufacture. The bubble soon burst. Post-war worldwide economic depression left Scotland with 28 per cent unemployment by 1932. Scottish slum conditions were among the worst in Britain.

Scotland's heavily industrialized society proved an ideal breeding ground for a militant labour movement. As head of the Scottish Miners' Federation, James Keir Hardie had founded the Scottish Labour Party in 1888. Pushing for ethical rather than Marxist socialism, it proved a vital force within the British Labour Party in the 20th century. The SLP's Ramsay Macdonald became Britain's first Labour prime minister in 1924 (though he was later disclaimed by his party when he formed a coalition with Conservatives and Liberals in 1931).

Scottish Government

The Scottish National Party was founded in 1934. Their campaign for Home Rule was interrupted by World War II and did not gather momentum again till the 1970s, when the discovery of North Sea oil whetted the appetite for Scottish sovereignty. In London, Margaret Thatcher's Tories opposed practically any degree of autonomy as a threat to the break-up of the United Kingdom. By 1997, the Tories lost all their Scottish seats in Westminster, and Tony Blair's Labour government pursued "Devolution" to provide limited self-government.

A Scottish general election in 1999 elected a 129-seat Scottish Parliament in Edinburgh with Labour leader Donald Dewar as the new First Minister. Work was begun on a new parliament building at Holyrood, where Scotland's earliest chronicled history began. It was inaugurated in October, 2004.

WARTIME FARCE

Scotland was the scene of one of the stranger events of World War II, when, on May 10, 1941, Hitler's deputy Rudolf Hess parachuted onto the estate of the Duke of Hamilton at Chatelherault Park just southwest of Glasgow. Having met Hamilton in Berlin at the 1936 Olympic Games, the mentally unstable Hess thought the duke might help with this personal peace feeler to the British government. Churchill found the news as crazy as the Marx Brothers film he was watching at the time. When he stopped laughing, the prime minister ordered Hess imprisoned in the Tower of London.

On the Scene

To "do" Scotland, taking in the main cities as well as something of the spectacular countryside, requires a car. Start out from Edinburgh, then explore its hinterland southeast across the Lothians and Scottish Borders—or begin in Glasgow, with a tour southwest across the Clyde to Ayrshire. Further north are the glens, castles and historic golf courses of Central Scotland. Argyll's west coast serves as a gateway to Arran and Kintyre. In northeast Scotland travel the Whisky Trail. The Highlands are the gateway to Skye, the Inner Hebrides and the Western Isles, or further north to Orkney and Shetland.

► EDINBURGH

Edinburgh Castle, Royal Mile, Holyrood,
New Town, Leith

The Scots are nothing if not proud, so they find it perfectly natural to place their prosperous and noble capital figuratively and literally on a pedestal. The residences of their rulers extend from the fortress of the medieval kings up on Castle Rock, an ancient volcanic hill, over to Holyrood, palace of the modern monarchs, and home of the brand new parliament of the Scottish government since 2004.

The city divides neatly into two parts: the Old and New Towns, separated by the boulevard-like Princes Street. The Old Town in turn is two worlds: that of the great castle, linked by the Royal Mile to Holyrood's palace and chapel, and, in a valley to the south, that of a warren of tenements in tiny blind-alley closes and courts, in large part renovated. New Town was built in open and airy style in the late 18th century. Further north is Leith, the city's port-district with its colourful waterfront on the Firth of Forth.

Edinburgh Castle

Dominating the skyline in mighty silhouette by day and illuminated at night, the great fortification up on the volcanic crag of Castle Rock provides the city with a perfect emblem. Though some kind of fort has stood on the rock for nearly 3000 years, it first entered historic records around AD 600 as *Dùn Eideann*, Gaelic for Eidyn's Fort, from which "Edinburgh" is derived. From the 12th to the 18th centuries it was a constant focus for the power struggles between Scottish and English kings.

Statues and Monuments

Enter the castle from the east side via the Esplanade, laid out in 1753 as a parade ground, scene now of the popular annual Edinburgh Military Tattoo. Among several military monuments is a bronze equestrian statue of Field Marshal Douglas Haig, Edinburgh-born commander of British forces in World War I.

The Gatehouse was built in the Romantic spirit of the 19th century, complete with drawbridge and two very feudal-looking statues of Scottish heroes, King Robert the Bruce on the left and William "Braveheart" Wallace on the right.

Beyond the formidable 16th-century Half Moon Battery to the west on Mill's Mount is the One O'Clock Gun. This World War II 25-pounder was fired originally for sailors in the Firth of Forth and now is a daily lunch-break signal for office-workers.

St Margaret's Chapel

This tiny Norman church is the castle's oldest surviving building, erected in the mid-12th century by King David I to honour his saintly mother Queen Margaret, wife of Malcolm III. It was rediscovered only in 1845 after serving 300 years as a gunpowder storehouse. This highest vantage point on Castle Rock offers a fine view north over Princes Street Gardens and the city's New Town.

The Palace

On Crown Square, within the castle grounds, the otherwise not very palatial palace possesses the splendid coronation regalia known as the Honours of Scotland. Together with an audio-visual presentation, the jewel-encrusted crown, sceptre and sword, all dating from the 16th century, are displayed in the Crown Room along with the venerable Stone of Destiny, the ancient seat on which the monarch was crowned.

Royal Mile

The Royal Mile slopes along the ridge from the Castle to the Palace of Holyroodhouse. Formed by Castlehill, Lawnmarket, High Street and Canongate, the immensely popular thoroughfare is lined with many fine refurbished houses and churches, but also some tacky souvenir shops. On either side, through archways known as pends, narrow closes (passages) lead to leafy courts of tenement houses transformed into desirable residences after years as foul-smelling slums.

The royal route runs longer than the English mile but almost exactly the length of the old mile of the Scots, who always liked more for their measures.

Castlehill

Castlehill boasts three top tourist attractions. At the Tartan Weaving Mill and Exhibition you can admire 150 different plaids and discover your own family tartan. The Scotch Whisky Heritage Centre tells the secrets of whisky-making with, naturally, tastings for adults. Not to forget the children, the 150-year-old Camera Obscura provides fascinating optical illusions and spectacular roof-top views over the city.

The Church of Scotland's nearby Assembly Hall was the temporary home of the new Scottish Parliament until its new quarters at Holyrood were completed.

Lawnmarket

At the old linen-market you can see two fine examples of 17th-century tenement housing.

The six-storey Gladstone's Land (belonging actually to the Gledstanes family), has a typical arcaded shopping booth on the ground floor.

Lady Stair's House has been converted into a Writer's Museum celebrating the life and work

---

STONE OF CONTENTION

The legendary Stone of Destiny is also known as the Stone of Scone, after the abbey in Perthshire where it was kept from 838 until stolen by Edward I of England in 1296 and taken to Westminster Abbey. Believed to be Jacob's Pillow on which the Hebrew patriarch dreamed of a ladder between heaven and earth, the sacred stone is said to have reached Scotland via the Holy Land, Spain and Ireland. It has served as a crowning seat for scores of Scottish and then English monarchs right down to the modern day. It was used in Queen Elizabeth II's coronation in 1953 and, after much controversy, returned to Scotland in 1996. Conspiracy buffs say the monks of Scone gave Edward a fake block of plain sandstone, while concealing the original, elaborately carved, nobody knows where. The abbey of Scone no longer exists.

HOIST WITH HIS OWN PETARD

Edinburgh is as proud of its rogues as it is of its heroes. On the south side of Lawnmarket, Brodie's Close is associated with the family of the infamous Deacon William Brodie. As a respectable citizen by day and fearsome burglar by night, he inspired Robert Louis Stevenson's *Dr Jekyll and Mr Hyde*. He was finally captured and executed—on gallows he himself had designed for the city and despite an iron collar he had hidden under his shirt.

of Robert Burns, Sir Walter Scott and Robert Louis Stevenson.

Church of St Giles

St Giles, High Kirk of Scotland, dominates the south side of High Street with its 15th-century spire fashioned by flying buttresses in the shape of the ancient Scottish crown. Medieval Edinburgh's parish church provided a platform for Scottish Reformation leader John Knox and in the 19th century commemorated other Scottish heroes with funerary monuments after the manner of Westminster Abbey. In the noble Gothic interior are some fine Pre-Raphaelite stained glass windows by William Morris and Edward Burne-Jones. The ornate Thistle Chapel in the southeast corner was added in 1911 for the 16 knights of the revered Order of the Thistle.

Museum of Childhood

At the lower end of High Street, the museum displays toys and games from all over the world, much to the squealing, yelling joy of its visitors.

Canongate

Many houses of this historically genteel residential neighbourhood have retained much of their 16th and 17th-century beauty, notably Chessel Court, Moray House (where the 1707 Act of Union was signed) and Huntly House, now a local history museum. Once a courthouse and prison, the Canongate Tollbooth now houses "The People's Story", a vivid permanent exhibition of everyday life and work in Edinburgh since the 18th century.

Holyrood

Holyrood's grand palace, romantic abbey ruin and magnificent park sit in a green and pleasant valley at the lower end of the Royal Mile. It's easy to understand why the Scottish monarchs progressively abandoned the bleak and draughty Castle Rock to move down here in the 16th century, after James IV built his palace near the Augustinian monastery founded by David I in 1128.

Palace of Holyroodhouse

Official residence of Queen Elizabeth II on her summer visits to Scotland, the palace is a largely baroque edifice transformed in the 17th century for Charles II—although he never lived there. The State Apartments open to the public preserve the chambers of Mary Queen of Scots (1542–67) in the palace's west corner tower at the top of a small, winding staircase. It was here that her husband Lord Darnley arranged the brutal murder (56 stab wounds) of her private secretary David Riccio, whom he believed to be the queen's lover. The Great Gallery, used today for royal receptions and investitures, is lined with 89 of the original 110 portraits by Jacob de Wit of Scotland's monarchs, legendary and real, from Fergus I to Charles II. Artistically more interesting is the Queen's Gallery opened in 2002 for changing exhibitions from the Royal Collection.

Holyrood Abbey

The beautiful ruined shell of the Gothic church offers eloquent testimony to the unending battle and strife between the Scots and English, devastating it over and over again, most notably in 1547 during the Reformation and again in the Revolution of 1688. The intricately carved porch of the western façade and twin towers indicate how splendid the abbey once was.

Holyrood Park

The royal park's greenery provides a breath of fresh air and exhilarating walks. Its 260 ha offer a delightful foretaste of much of Scotland's varied land-

HIGHLIGHTS

- **Edinburgh Castle**: Scotland's most historic fortress
- **Holyrood**: royal palace, abbey-ruin and new Parliament
- **Museum of Scotland**: superb modern museum of Scotland's ancient story
- **Princes Street Gardens**: charming park with view of Castle and Old Town
- **Charlotte Square**: Britain's finest Georgian architecture
- **Leith**: great waterfront pubs, seafood restaurants and *Britannia* royal yacht

DAVID AND THE STAG

In time-honoured manner, Holyrood Abbey's foundation is attributed to a miracle. David I is said to have avoided being gored to death by a stag when its antlers were transformed into a holy cross (rood), prompting the pious king to build a monastery on the spot. Canongate's coat of arms commemorates this sacred event with the emblematic stag's head with a holy cross between its antlers.

scapes—craggy mountain country, marshes, moorland, lochs, glens and meadows. East of the palace, the Queen's Drive loop-road leads clockwise past St Margaret's Loch, an artificial pond beside a ruin of 15th-century St Anthony's Chapel. Continue south to the park beyond Dunsapie Loch. A signposted footpath leads up a grassy slope for an easygoing 20-minute walk to the park's highest point, Arthur's Seat (250 m). From this volcanic rock, look south over the Pentland Hills, north to the Firth of Forth and, on the proverbial clear day, to the Highlands 130 km away. (For the Arthur in question, only an obscure 6th-century Prince Arthur of Strathclyde has been suggested in place of the unlikely King of Camelot.)

Among the park's dramatic rock formations are the Lion's Haunch and Samson's Ribs on the southern edge and the Salisbury Crags to the west, said to have inspired Edinburgh scholar James Hutton (1726–97) to pioneer the noble science of geology. His ideas and those of his followers are expounded in the popular "Our Dynamic Earth" exhibit on Holyrood Road, in a renovated brewery topped by a tensioned fabric membrane (with a good view of the new Scottish Parliament).

Scottish Parliament

This spectacular modern complex sprawls at the foot of the Royal Mile, opposite the palace of Holyrood. Catalan architect Enric Miralles created a hemispheric debating chamber that avoids the more confrontational design of London's rectangular House of Commons. Access to the building is free and it's open every weekday; the best days for viewing its ambitious design and joining a guided tour are Mondays and Fridays, or other days when Parliament is in recess. Phone ahead on 0131 348 5200.

Around the corner is The Tun, a redeveloped brick warehouse on Holyrood Road with a striking concrete and green copper extension leaning over the street. It houses offices, with a bar and café on the ground floor.

22

Scotland's controversial new Parliament complex has proved to be a popular tourist attraction.

Cowgate and Grassmarket

Extending west of Holyrood Road and running parallel to the Royal Mile, the thoroughfare formed by Cowgate and Grassmarket brought together the city's seamy underworld in bars and brothels—and provided public gallows for their hangings. The whole neighbourhood is now being renovated to create a more salubrious but still lively atmosphere of art galleries, boutiques, cafés and restaurants and less seedy bars and nightclubs.

Museum of Scotland

One of Britain's finest new museums stands on Chambers Street in a splendid modern building appropriate to its lively and imaginative presentation of Scotland's fascinating identity. The cylindrical tower in honey-coloured sandstone offers a handsome emblematic landmark. Combining original artefacts and state-of-the-art audio-visual effects, the museum tells Scotland's story from its geological and prehistoric beginnings, through the turbulent and creative times of its wars and world-shaking contributions to industrial revolution, up to the modern day achievements of people as varied as Prime Minister Tony Blair and film actor Sean Connery.

23

Royal Museum of Scotland

Nearby, in a more sedate, glass-roofed Victorian building, this museum presents a wide-ranging collection of treasures from all over the world, antiquities and latterly creations from Asia, Europe and the Americas.

New Town

The area stretching north from what is now Princes Street was laid out over two centuries ago to let citizens, at least the more prosperous ones, escape the increasingly cramped quarters of Old Town. The bright and spacious urban grid plan designed by James Craig and Robert Adam provides a showcase for some of Britain's most exquisite Georgian (neoclassical) architecture.

Princes Street

With the busy and unimaginative department stores that have replaced most of its 18th-century buildings, the main thoroughfare does not make an auspicious architectural introduction to New Town. At the east end, there's a lonely dignity to Robert Adam's noble Register House (1774), keeper of Scotland's historic records. Otherwise, the street is saved by its great views of the Castle and Old Town and the lovely Princes Street Gardens. Towering over it is the Scott Monument, with its statue of Sir Walter, his dog Maida, 64 characters from his novels, 16 fellow Scots authors and 287 steps to the top of the majestic Gothic pile.

National Gallery of Scotland

In the East Princes Gardens, the neo-Grecian National Gallery houses Scotland's premier art collection of European masters, including Rembrandt, Vermeer and Rubens; Raphael, Titian, Tintoretto and Veronese; Cranach and Holbein; Hugo van der Goes and Quentin Metsys; Velázquez, Zurbarán and Goya; Watteau, Gauguin, Cézanne and Monet; and Scotland's own Henry Raeburn.

George Street

With stately Charlotte Square at one end and St Andrew Square at the other, George Street, lined with 18th-century mansions, is the centrepiece of New Town. Many of the mansions are now in the hands of banks or other financial institutions, others house fashionable boutiques, and stylish bars and restaurants. Opposite the oval-plan church of St Andrew and St George are the Assembly Rooms (1787), venue for Charles Dickens's public readings and now for Fringe groups of the Edinburgh Festival.

The magnificent building of the Royal Bank of Scotland stands on St Andrew Square.

Charlotte Square
Designed in 1791, a year before his death, Charlotte Square is Robert Adam's splendid architectural swan song, regarded by many as the finest Georgian square in Britain. Bute House at No. 6 is the home of the Scottish Parliament's First Minister. The lower floors of No. 7 constitute the National Trust for Scotland's Georgian House (1796), presenting to the public classical interiors of the period, including dining room, kitchen and wine cellar. (Trust headquarters are at No. 28, next to its gourmet restaurant, Taste of Scotland.)

Queen Street
The mansions on this best-preserved of New Town's three main streets are still privately owned, with owners each holding a key to the gardens on the north side of the street. The Scottish National Portrait Gallery at the east end celebrates Scotland's greats, from Bonnie Prince Charlie and Mary Queen of Scots to philosopher David Hume and Manchester United football manager Alex Ferguson.

Royal Botanic Garden
On Inverleith Row just north of New Town, the Royal Botanic Garden covers 28 ha. It boasts azaleas and rhododendrons, Chinese flowers, great stands of oak, lime, maple and rowan, and a courtyard of Alpine flowers in front of the lofty Victorian Palm House. A trail of temperate and tropical flora leads to palm-like cycad plants that date back to the era of the dinosaurs.

Leith
Seafood restaurants and bright and breezy pubs have turned Edinburgh's harbourfront district into a major tourist attraction. After centuries as Scotland's main east-coast port, Leith was incorporated into Edinburgh in 1920, becoming a seedy and even downright dangerous slum until its transformation in the 1980s. Neoclassical tenements have been refurbished along the Water of Leith canal. The old Town Hall on Constitution Street is now the most handsome of police stations. To the east, the park of Leith Links is said to have been a golf course in the 15th century, which would make it the true birthplace of Scotland's sporting gift to the world.

Britannia
Moored off Ocean Drive in the Port of Leith's Western Harbour, the royal yacht *Britannia* (decommissioned in 1997) now attracts a paying public to inspect its five decks, including royal dining room, sitting room, sun lounge and engine room.

The region south and east of Edinburgh takes in the Lothians from the Firth of Forth and North Sea coast, over the Lammermuir Hills to the counties of the Scottish Borders straddling the Tweed Valley down to England. In this inevitable battlefield of wars between English and Scots, ruined castles and abbeys are the countryside's landmarks. In quieter times, the Adam family of architects produced some of their finest country houses here, and Sir Walter Scott made his home at Melrose.

The Lothians

Named after King Lot, brother-in-law of King Arthur, the region is divided administratively into East Lothian, Midlothian and West Lothian. (The football team Heart of Midlothian bears the name of an old Edinburgh prison, demolished long ago.) The attractions here are all close enough to Edinburgh to make an easy day trip.

Hopetoun House

On the banks of the Forth, just west of its two great road and rail bridges, the Earl of Hopetoun's 18th-century residence is truly palatial. It was designed by William Bruce, architect of Holyroodhouse, greatly expanded by William Adam, and lavishly decorated in its interior by his son, Robert, master builder of Edinburgh's New Town. The great curving sweep of the façade is reminiscent of Roman baroque, a tone sustained inside by the exuberant Red and Yellow Drawing Rooms. The parkland around the house is open to the public for walks and picnics.

Linlithgow

At the edge of Linlithgow Loch, 10 km (6 miles) west of Edinburgh, the largely 15th-century palace was gutted by fire, but the present-day roofless ruin, still handsome, is a delight for children and adults alike to explore for the sudden surprising open-air vistas at the top of its spiral staircases. The highest vantage point is the Queen's Tower in the northwest corner. The palace was the birthplace of James V (1512) and his daughter, Mary Queen of Scots (1542); Bonnie Prince Charlie stopped here during the uprising of 1745. The palace caught fire a year later, when it was occupied by English troops.

26

The Cistercian abbey of Melrose stands in eloquent ruin.

Rosslyn Chapel

Just 5 km (3 miles) south of Edinburgh's city centre, this magnificently decorated Gothic chapel stands in the town of Roslin (also famous for the institute that produced Dolly, the world's first cloned sheep). Founded in 1446 by William St Clair and intended originally to be part of a great collegiate church, the chapel is a masterpiece of the mason's and sculptor's art, particularly on the pillars and their capitals. The beautifully carved Apprentice Pillar is said to have been done during his master's absence, prompting such a fit of jealous rage that the master killed the apprentice with a mallet.

NICE TRY, BUT NO

The iconography of Rosslyn Chapel's carvings is full of enigmas, several of them associated with masonic, pagan and other esoteric symbolism which Dan Brown worked into his best-seller, *The Da Vinci Code*. Among the representations of plants, two are identified as maize and aloe cactus from the Americas, supporting a theory that the founder's seafaring grandfather Prince Henry of Orkney had crossed the Atlantic 100 years before Columbus. Sadly, local scholars now believe that these carvings were added in the 16th century.

North Berwick

The drive from Edinburgh takes you through a string of picturesque golf links on the way to this pleasant old-fashioned Victorian beach resort on the North Sea coast. Some of its history from the Middle Ages to the present day is told in the town museum housed in the old parish school, but the main attraction is the fascinating Scottish Seabird Centre opened in 2000. From here, thousands of seabirds—gannets, puffins, guillemots, razorbills and terns—can be observed out on nearby Bass Rock and Fidra Island. Visitors can view them not only through powerful telescopes but also via remote-controlled TV cameras concealed on the craggy sanctuaries. Other cameras are installed on the Isle of May, 17 km (10 miles) further north (which also has a large colony of breeding grey seals). There have been increasingly regular sightings of bottle-nosed dolphins with their calves in the Firth of Forth, as well as minke and humpback whales.

At Tantallon Castle, 5 km (3 miles) east of North Berwick, the clifftop ruins offer spectacular views of Bass Rock, where the Douglases, Earls of Angus, hunted gannet for their supper.

Dunbar

The little fishing port, with a charming double harbour, is best known as birthplace of the great naturalist John Muir (1838–1914), a founder of America's national parks system. John Muir House, 128 High Street, tells the story of his boyhood in Dunbar and his life's work setting up the Sequoia and Yosemite national parks. In his honour, the John Muir Country Park has been established a short walk from the harbour around Belhaven Bay and along the rugged East Lothian coast, taking in the ruins of Dunbar Castle.

Haddington

There is a sedate charm to this prosperous country town on the River Tyne, resting happily on laurels won by its gentlemen farmers as pioneers of the 18th-century Agricultural Revolution. The fruit of their innovations in machinery, seeding and stock-breeding can be seen in the handsome gabled houses along the triangle formed by tree-lined Court Street, High Street, Hardgate and Market Street.

South of the town centre, St Mary's is Scotland's largest parish church, notable in its interior for superb 16th-century canopied alabaster tombs in the Lauderdale Aisle.

Lammermuir Hills

This flat-topped low-lying range of hills watered by small streams marks the frontier between East Lothian and The Borders. Just south of Haddington is the pretty little 18th-century hamlet of Gifford. It makes a good starting point for ramblers to take several well-marked footpaths that meet up with the Southern Upland Way running east from Lauder to Cocksburnpath on the North Sea coast. Many of the footpaths follow historic drovers' and carters' trails to and from England.

The Scottish Borders

The Borders cover the Southern Uplands of heather-covered hills, fast-flowing rivers and bleak, windswept moorland between the

---

HIGHLIGHTS

- **Linlithgow Palace**: castle ruin with great views
- **Rosslyn Chapel**: superb carvings steeped in legend
- **North Berwick Scottish Seabird Centre**: bird-watchers' paradise
- **Melrose Abbey**: one of Sir Walter Scott's favourites

29

The 3000 volumes in the library of Traquair House are catalogued according to a code system based on the portraits above the shelves.

Lammermuirs and the Cheviot Hills in Northumberland, across the River Tweed. From Peebles southeast to Melrose, the stately houses of the market towns and the romantic abbeys contrast with the densely wooded Tweed Valley in the centre of the region.

Peebles

This easy-going town sits astride the Tweed, 45 minutes' drive south of Edinburgh. Surrounded by forested slopes, it makes a good base for exploring the valley. Among the many attractive Victorian houses on the broad High Street is the Tweeddale Museum, a gift of William Chambers, the founding publisher of the famous encyclopaedia. In the museum are stucco frieze copies of the Elgin Marbles and a 19th-century *Triumph of Alexander*.

Traquair House

Situated across the river from the village of Innerleithen, Traquair is believed to be the oldest continuously inhabited residence in Britain, the Maxwell Stuart lairds having lived here since 1491. Kings, queens and refugee priests have passed through, but the house has never lost its warm atmosphere. Beautifully furnished drawing room, stately bedrooms, dining room, library and chapel are there to be admired, but so, too, is the housekeeper's simple "still room" where she would relax between calls to service. In the grounds, a maze has been newly planted and an 18th-century brewery resurrected to produce the much appreciated Traquair House Ale. Beyond is parkland of oaks and pines.

Melrose

The charming town of Melrose lies on the banks of the Tweed with three peaks of the Eildon Hills making a dramatic backdrop. Quaint little cottages alternate with lofty dignified Georgian and Victorian terrace houses. Its customary tranquillity is broken only by the Rugby Sevens Week in April, a tradition dating back to 1883 when Melrose created this spirited version of an already highly spirited sport. Just behind Market Square, the noble ruin of Melrose Abbey (founded by David I in 1136) still stands, despite the best efforts of England's Richard II in 1386 and Henry VIII in 1545 to destroy it. The late-Gothic Cistercian abbey-church dates from the 14th and 15th centuries. The many finely sculpted architectural details and grotesque gargoyles include, on the south side of the nave, a pig playing the bagpipes. The heart of Robert the Bruce was buried here, rediscovered in a lead casket in 1996 and now kept in the nearby Commendator's House.

Abbotsford House

East of Melrose, the house where Sir Walter Scott lived from 1812 till his death in 1832 has become a veritable shrine to the Great Man and the Scotland to which he devoted his life and work. Scott renovated and extended the farmhouse he bought here with a fanciful hodgepodge of styles he admired in other Scottish monuments—the porch of Linlithgow Palace, Melrose Abbey's cloister, sundry battlements, turrets and step-gabled façades from all over the place. In the library, along with Scott's own 9000 rare books, is an astonishing collection of relics—a lock of Bonnie Prince Charlie's hair, Robert Burns's drinking cup and Rob Roy's purse. His broadsword, dirk and sporran are in the Armoury.

Dryburgh Abbey

Sir Walter Scott chose to be buried in the ruin of this medieval monastery surrounded by venerable cedar trees, amid hills east of Melrose. It was founded in the 12th century by austere Premonstratensian (White Canon) monks from Northumberland and frequently rebuilt. Near the grave of Scott in the northern transept of the abbey-church is that of Field Marshal Haig.

31

GLASGOW

City Centre, East End, Around the Cathedral,
West End, South of the River Clyde

Glasgow's urban face, for better or for worse, has in many ways been the face of modern Scotland itself. Right now, most of it is looking good. The spirited, cheerful Glaswegians have swept aside their town's old image of dreary industrial metropolis to show off the great architecture, splendid museums and theatres, fine restaurants and—who are we to argue?—the best pubs in the world. Its culture may be less cosmopolitan than that of Edinburgh, but perhaps more triumphantly Scottish, its citizens less decorous but more exuberant. Although it has lost to the suburbs and new districts almost half the population that topped 1 million in the 1930s, Glasgow remains Scotland's largest city, with 579,000 inhabitants in the 2001 census, to Edinburgh's 450,000.

City Centre

The buildings of the district north of the River Clyde and east of the M8 motorway, with George Square at its centre, prompted poet and architectural critic John

In the Hunterian you can admire Charles Rennie Mackintosh's bedroom.

Betjeman to call Glasgow "the greatest Victorian city in the world". Walking is the best way around this compact area, now beautifully refurbished, while the Underground provides an easy link to the city's West End.

George Square

The town's main square is an appropriate showcase for Glaswegian civic pride in the achievements of its great 19th century. The column in the centre is topped by a statue of Walter Scott, surrounded by monuments to other Scottish heroes and British dignitaries, prime among them an equestrian statue of Queen Victoria herself, particularly popular as she came to prefer Scotland to England.

Glasgow City Chambers

No mere "town hall", only the more dignified name of Glasgow City Chambers could be suitable for William Young's lofty neo-Renaissance building that is the seat of municipal government. Dominating the east side of George Square, it was inaugurated by Queen Victoria in 1888 when Glasgow was the second city of her British Empire. The friezes on the façade glorify the   33 enthroned queen, the colonies, the four countries of the United Kingdom and the allegories of the principles they were all expected to extol—Knowledge, Virtue and Religion. On a free guided tour of the opulent gilt and marble interior, you can see the imperial point hammered home by its mosaics, monumental staircase and soaring pillars.

Merchants' House

On the northwest corner of George Square stands the grand Merchants' House, built by John Burnet in 1874 and now housing Glasgow's Chamber of Commerce. It is topped by a domed tower on which is perched a globe with a gilded square-rigged sailing Ship of Commerce plying its seas, symbolizing the worldwide trade in which the merchants were involved.

Merchant City

Southeast of George Square, the 18th-century warehouses and 19th-century trading houses have been spruced up to accommodate art galleries, fashionable boutiques, bars and cafés on the ground floor, with chic loft apartments on the higher floors.

At its Glasgow headquarters in the elegant Hutchesons' Hall (1802), 158 Ingram Street, the National Trust for Scotland offers Merchant City Trail leaflets and audio-guides to landmarks in the neighbourhood, as well as a permanent *Glasgow Style* exhibition devoted to local art trends.

The Italian Centre at the corner of Ingram and John streets is an example of the switch from warehouse to stylish shops and cafés.

With its distinctive green copper dome, Trades House on Glassford Street is the only Glasgow building of Georgian architect Robert Adam, completed in 1794, two years after his death. It was originally built for 14 trade guilds, including bakers, weavers, bonnet makers and shipwrights, and still serves their charitable activities. It can be visited by arrangement.

Gallery of Modern Art

On Royal Exchange Square, this controversial gallery is located somewhat incongruously in what was originally a tobacco baron's extravagant 18th-century home. On four floors said to correspond to the natural elements of Earth, Water, Fire and Air, it exhibits works by Niki de Saint Phalle, Andy Warhol, David Hockney, Brazilian photographer Sebastião Salgado and, most interestingly, Scottish avant-garde artists such as Ken Currie, Peter Howson, and Adrian Wiszniewski. On the top floor is a dedicated Education and Access studio, with workshops and artists' talks.

The Lighthouse

West of Buchanan Street on Mitchell Lane, the Lighthouse is Scotland's Centre for Architecture, Design and the City. It was transformed from the old *Glasgow Herald* building, Charles Rennie Mackintosh's first public commission in 1895. Now named the Mackintosh Tower, the building's landmark chubby corner turret originally served as a water-tower to cope with the newspaper's fire-prone printing presses. Today, a new spiral staircase takes visitors up inside the tower through the main stages of the architect's life and work, with great city views from the top. There are also first-class temporary exhibitions of architecture and design.

Sauchiehall Street

Running west from the huge Royal Concert Hall and Buchanan Galleries Shopping Centre, Sauchiehall (rhymes with hockey

RESURRECTION

Glasgow has picked itself up, dusted itself off and overcome years of depression to make the city an amazingly enjoyable place to be. Amazing because so few thought it possible. In the 18th century, the city had thrived on trade with Europe and the Americas, exporting textiles, coal and fish and importing sugar, rum and tobacco. Energetic manufacturers on the River Clyde turned iron, chemicals and shipbuilding into the grimy gold of 19th-century Scotland's Industrial Revolution. The entrepreneurs built themselves some of Britain's finest Victorian housing, stately mansions and lofty tenements (not a pejorative word in those days), with a great social and cultural life to go with them. This was the age of Glasgow's best-known architect and brilliant furniture designer, Charles Rennie Mackintosh. Then, in the aftermath of World War I, prosperity ground to a halt and the name of Glasgow soon evoked little more than grey and gloomy slums.

The city moped along until the 1980s, when an enlightened civic leadership came up with a slogan, "Glasgow's Miles Better", that has proved to be a self-fulfilling prophecy. The soot and gloom have been scraped away to restore the tenements to their original buff and plum-red sandstone beauty. Old warehouses have been transformed into new galleries, theatres and museums. The idea of declaring Glasgow "European City of Culture" in 1990 was a joke only to those who had not been there. Nine years later came the added accolade of "City of Architecture and Design".

35

ball) Street is Gaelic for "alley of the willows". This inspired Charles Rennie Mackintosh and his wife Margaret to use willow motifs for the famous Willow Tea Rooms, now faithfully reconstructed upstairs at No. 217. The gentle curves of the willow serve to offset the interior's otherwise very angular design.

With Glasgow's special taste for mixing ancient and modern, the Centre for Contemporary Arts (350 Sauchiehall) stages its exhibitions, performance arts and art-house films in the refurbished Grecian Chambers office building designed in 1865 by Alexander "Greek" Thomson, as he was understandably known.

Glasgow School of Art
North of Sauchiehall, it's a steep climb up Dalhousie to 167 Renfrew Street, but well worth it to see the generally acknowledged summit of Charles Rennie Mackintosh's architectural achievement. Completed in two phases —the main building in 1899 and a west wing added in 1909—the still functioning Glasgow School of Art cannily combines past and present in its massive façade. Elements from the Scottish castle and manor-house tradition blend with modern use of metalwork, Mackintosh's characteristic rectangles, and the natural curves of Art Nouveau.

Inside, enthusiastic art school students conduct guided tours of a building in which Mackintosh designed every detail to ensure they would enjoy proper working conditions after his own cramped experience in the old art school on Sauchiehall. Art studios are flooded with the light of tall north-facing windows. In the

HIGHLIGHTS

- **George Square**: showcase for Glasgow's 19th-century heyday
- **Glasgow School of Art**: Charles Rennie Mackintosh's masterpiece
- **People's Palace**: entertaining view of the city's social realities
- **Hunterian Art Gallery**: great paintings by James McNeill Whistler and "Glasgow Boys"
- **Burrell Collection**: shipping magnate's astonishingly eclectic art treasures

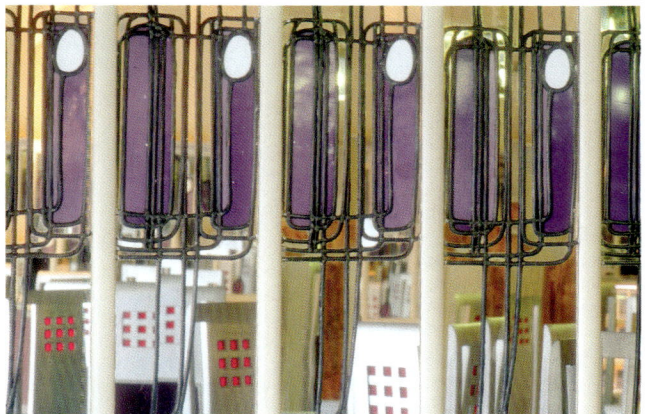

Mackintosh designed every aspect of the Willow Tea Rooms, from the leaded glass screens and chairs to the teaspoons and waitress's dresses.

magnificent two-storey library, he designed every bookshelf, curved chair, reading table and light-fixture. He even put colour-coded glazed tiling in the corridors to guide teachers and students though the vast building. Earlier furniture can be seen in the Mackintosh Room, while the Furniture Gallery at the top of the school displays superb originals of his high-backed chairs, chests of drawers and bedroom suites.

The Tenement House

Northwest of the School of Art, downhill on Buccleuch Street, the National Trust for Scotland has preserved at No. 145 a touching example of Glasgow's tenement housing in the first half of the 20th century. The original home of Agnes Toward and her mother is presented in every loving detail, with all the furniture, dishes, pots and pans, personal letters, postcards, holiday photos and shop-bills accumulated over a lifetime from 1911 to 1965.

East End

Saltmarket and High Street mark the eastern edge of Merchant City. Beyond that, the East End still epitomizes the grim popular image of old Glasgow. This is the remnant of the densely populated area inhabited by the workers 37

CLAPPIE DOOS?

The People's Palace provides a very useful guide to Glaswegian English, so often a mystery to visitors, with a little recorded help from comedians Billy Connolly and Dorothy Paul. We learn that *zarra facmac* means "is that so?", *breeks* are trousers, *wean* are children, *bunnet* a cap, *jorries* are marbles and *clappie doos* are mussels. If you don't understand, whatever you do, don't *throw a flaky*—get upset.

who produced the wealth that built the architectural splendours of the city centre. Depression of the 1920s and 30s shut down the factories and until recently only a few sad cafés, pubs and shops remained. But today regeneration is underway with the construction of housing and leisure facilities.

The Barras

The Barras is the local name for the barrows and stalls that make up the city's biggest, bustling weekend market, sprawling through the cobbled alleys and streets south of Gallowgate. Here, the huge red gates are only a nominal entrance to the market. Some people come for the new and second-hand clothes and gadgets, or to sift among the bric-a-brac and junk where they might even find the occasional genuine antique—but most are here to soak up the cheerful atmosphere.

Glasgow Green

South of London Road, the green stretching down to the River Clyde has been the citizens' common since the Middle Ages and is believed to be Britain's oldest public park. In addition to a pleasant stroll not unlike the Italians' *passeggiata*, a few Glaswegians still exercise their right to hang and dry their washing here. The Green has many historical associations: Bonnie Prince Charlie paraded his troops here in 1745; the Chartists staged mass demonstrations in the 1830s; and workers ended their May Day marches here up until the 1950s. British, if not Scottish, patriotism is asserted by a monument to Lord Nelson, 44 m (144 ft) high.

People's Palace

At the north end of the Green, this once rather austere Victorian folk museum has been lovingly renovated to present a lively picture of Glasgow's industrial and social life. While much is treated with humour, exhibits also confront uncomfortable subjects like the abuse of alcohol and the rivalry of The Old Firm supporters of Rangers and Celtic football clubs. Ken Currie's modern murals offer a radical account of striking weavers in the 18th century and more recent Clydeside militants in this hot bed of Scottish socialism. A prominent place is also given to Glasgow's capitalist and industrial heroes, including tea-magnate Thomas Lipton, publisher William Collins and James Beaumont Neilson, who invented hot blast furnaces for iron smelting. Home life in the tenements and one-roomed houses is displayed in a vivid sound-and-light show.

Around the Cathedral

On the east side of town at the north end of High Street, the cathedral is built on the site of Glasgow's original settlement.

Glasgow Cathedral

Dedicated to St Mungo, the city's patron saint, the cathedral is a largely 13th-century Gothic edifice. Its two outstanding architectural elements are the stone tracery of the 15th-century choir screen and the masterfully executed fan vaulting down in the crypt, which contains St Mungo's tomb.

The stained glass windows are nearly all modern. The church's sculpture and other medieval ornament were destroyed by 16th-century Protestant Reformation zeal against "idolatry"—after its last Catholic archbishop had fled to France with much of the cathedral treasure.

Necropolis

Offering a fine view of the cathedral from the rear, and reached by a Bridge of Sighs, the Necropolis is modelled on the Paris cemetery of Père Lachaise, but built on a

---

MUNGO'S MIRACLES

Mungo, the man on Glasgow's coat of arms, is believed to have been the city's 6th-century founder. Mungo was his nickname, perhaps meaning "My Hound", his real name being the more decorous Kentigern, "Chief Lord"—but this is Glasgow. The bell on the coat of arms is a papal gift to call the faithful to prayer. The other emblems represent the three miracles needed in the Middle Ages to qualify for sainthood. The fish is a salmon that Mungo caught in the River Clyde with a royal wedding ring in its belly, thus saving from execution a repentant adulterous queen. The bird is a robin killed by Mungo's schoolmates, but resuscitated by the future saint. The tree symbolizes a frozen hazel branch which Mungo managed to set alight by prayer when the holy fire of his monastery was put out by those incorrigible classmates.

hill. Its elaborate monumental tombs and mausoleums honour the memory of Glasgow's merchant aristocracy and form an eerie skyline. At the summit is a monument to John Knox.

St Mungo Museum

To give it its full name, the St Mungo Museum of Religious Life and Art is devoted to the art and cult objects of the world's major religions—including a Zen Buddhist rock and gravel garden outside, paintings and stained-glass windows inside. Modern art lovers come to see Salvador Dali's astonishing *Christ of St John of the Cross*, a "God's eye-view" of the Crucifixion bought by the city in 1951. It will be returned to Kelvingrove Art Gallery in summer 2006.

Provand's Lordship

The simple stone house opposite the museum is the oldest in Glasgow, built in 1471 for a prebendary clergyman ("provand"). After serving as part of a hospice for the poor, it later became a tavern and brothel. The ground-floor furnishings and the paintings upstairs illustrate the house's colourful history.

At the rear, the St Nicholas Garden was laid out in 1997 to grow medicinal plants used in the 15th century during the house's more charitable period.

West End

Beyond the M8 motorway, the airy and bright area with Kelvingrove Park and Glasgow University at its heart has been the home of choice of the city's bourgeoisie since the 19th century. Families of the industrialists and entrepreneurs fled the grime of the city centre and East End to build their fine mansions, handsome tenements and terraced housing around the greenery along the meandering River Kelvin.

The university abandoned its confined quarters near the cathedral to move here in 1870. Major museums sprang up in the wake of international exhibitions. Today, Byres Road, between the Hillhead and Kelvin Hall Underground stations, is the main thoroughfare for the West End's best pubs, cafés, restaurants and smarter shops.

Hunterian Art Gallery

On the north side of Glasgow University at 82 Hillhead Street, the Hunterian Art Gallery is best known for its James McNeill Whistler collection, the largest outside the United States. Most remarkable among the 80 oil paintings (in addition to several hundred drawings and watercolours) are the portraits of women. The gallery also displays the American artist's personal possessions—furniture, silver, ceramics and artist's materials. There are important European paintings by Rembrandt, Rubens, Boudin and Pissarro, but of particular interest are the Scottish works of the "Glasgow Boys", notably James Guthrie, George Henry and Edward Atkinson Hornel.

Mackintosh House
For the Mackintosh House, in an adjacent gallery, the Hunterian has lovingly reconstructed the hall, dining room, studio-drawing room and main bedroom from the home where Charles Rennie Mackintosh and his artist wife Margaret lived from 1906 to 1914. The original house was demolished in 1963 because of subsidence, but the Hunterian was able to salvage most of its fittings and decorate the re-created house with original Mackintosh furniture. Even the bric-a-brac, fitted carpets, curtains and other soft furnishings are faithful to contemporary descriptions and photographs of the house.

Kelvingrove Museum and Art Gallery
Originally built to house the International Exhibition of 1901, the museum is currently being refurbished and due to reopen in summer 2006. Until then, the monumental red sandstone building itself is worth a quick look as a splendid example of the grandiose Scottish baronial style affected by Glasgow's industrial princes. The renovation includes stripping modern fittings to reveal the Victorian architecture beneath.

Part of the collections can be seen at the Open Museum at Nitshill, just south of Glasgow. This is a storage facility and resource centre in an industrial estate, where members of the public can browse the shelves on a free guided tour, daily at 2.30 p.m. The Kelvingrove reserve collection will remain here after the reopening. For more information see www.glasgowmuseums.com/kelvingrove/

Transport Museum
In the grounds of Kelvin Hall, this huge museum displays every kind of transport—historic locomotives, trams, vintage cars, a Spitfire fighter plane from World War II, circus caravans, fire engines, children's prams and what is believed to be the world's oldest surviving pedal cycle. A particularly popular exhibit is the Clyde Room of 250 ship models from Glasgow's 19th-century merchant sailing vessels to the first steamships and the grand ocean-going liners that made the Clyde ship works world-famous: the three Queens, Mary, Elizabeth and Elizabeth II. "Kelvin

41

Street" is a charming recreation of a 1950s cobbled street with a butcher, a baker, an Italian coffee shop and an old-fashioned Underground station.

The Tall Ship
at Glasgow Harbour

Moored on Yorkhill Quay, down on the River Clyde, the three-masted *Glenlee* invites visitors to come aboard one of the five Clyde-built sailing ships still afloat. Launched in 1896, this noble relic tells the story of Glasgow's great shipbuilding era. Other exhibits can be seen at the nearby Pumphouse. You can also take a cruise on the Clyde on the Tall Ship's river-bus, the *Frances Mary*.

SECC

Part of the Queen's Dock redevelopment project, the Scottish Exhibition and Conference Centre is noteworthy for its gleaming SECC & Clyde auditorium designed by Sir Norman Foster and affectionately called the Armadillo. Used for all kinds of events, it was inaugurated in 1997.

South of the River Clyde

Immediately across the river from the Exhibition Centre is the new Glasgow Science Centre. Beyond the depressed Govan district and Glasgow Rangers' Ibrox stadium are the genteel suburbs around the greenery of Pollok Park and Queens Park. Here you will find one of Glasgow's finest museums and architectural gems associated with Mackintosh and Alexander "Greek" Thomson.

Glasgow Science Centre (gsc)

Opened on the south bank of the Clyde by Queen Elizabeth in 2001, the Glasgow Science Centre has at its heart the spectacular crescent-shaped titanium-clad Science Mall. Exhibits are devoted to contemporary and future developments in science and technology. With the gsc's staff of trained scientists on hand to help and advise, the emphasis is on hands-on displays, online facilities, interactive workshops and live science shows. Major features are a state-of-the-art planetarium and gigantic IMAX theatre showing both two- and three-dimensional films. The Glasgow Tower, 105 m (345 ft) high and designed to revolve through 360° from the ground up, offers a spectacular view from the observation deck—but check in advance to make sure the lifts are working.

The Burrell Collection

Beautifully situated in Pollok Park 5 km (3 miles) southwest of the city centre, the Burrell Collection is housed in a modern building opened in 1983 for the huge eclectic array of art treasures amassed by shipping magnate William Burrell. A covered courtyard displays bronze sculptures by Rodin and Jacob Epstein, along with the monumental Roman "Warwick" Vase (2nd century AD).

Antiquities grouped together in the Ancient Civilizations collection feature art from Mesopotamia, Egypt, Greece and Rome. The Medieval collection includes tapestries, silverware and glassware, but also, all incorporated into the building's fabric, monumental Romanesque portals, Gothic stone tracery, an English alabaster altarpiece and splendid German Rhenish stained-glass windows. Among the exhibits of European painting are works by Rembrandt, Giovanni Bellini, Degas, Pissaro, Cézanne and Manet.

Pollok House

Across the park southwest of the Burrell Collection, this sturdy but elegant country manor was designed by William Adam in 1752 for the Maxwell family, resident in Pollok from 1269 to 1966. Besides paintings by William Blake, it has a good collection of Spanish art—El Greco, Murillo and Goya. Amid lovely rhododendron gardens with the little White Cart river running through it, the house itself is the main attraction, as an example of gracious country living. Visitors can roam at will through library and billiard room, and take a break "below stairs" where the servants' parlour is now a tea room serving fine home baking.

House for an Art Lover

North of Pollok, in Bellahouston Park, the house was built 1989–1996 from a design that Charles and Margaret Mackintosh entered for a competition held by a German magazine in 1901. The top two floors are used by the Glasgow School of Art, but other rooms are open to the public—the stunning white Music Room (note the piano!), a tiled and wood-panelled Dining Room, and the Oval Room to which ladies retired while the men partook of cigars and brandy.

Holmwood House

Perched on the banks of the River Cart, in suburban Cathcart, 6 km (4 miles) south of the city centre, Holmwood House (61–63 Netherlee Road) has been nicely restored to present a showcase for the Hellenic tastes of 19th-century architect Alexander "Greek" Thomson. The opulent villa's drawing room, parlour and dining room are richly decorated in marble, mahogany and plaster, including a frieze of scenes from Homer's *Iliad*.

43

Southwest Scotland was known in medieval times just as Galloway. With its thriving ports serving ships on the Solway Firth, it was often a source of conflict between the English and its defiantly independent chieftains. That strife has left many romantic castle ruins, but the region is now one of Scotland's more tranquil corners, typified by the picturesque town of Kirkcudbright. It is also much appreciated by poetry pilgrims as the home of Robbie Burns, who was born in Alloway on the Ayrshire coast and mostly remembered for penning the traditional New Year's Eve song *Auld Lang Syne* ("times past").

Dumfries
On the River Nith just north of the Solway Firth, Dumfries was known in the Middle Ages as the "Queen of the South", when it was a prosperous trading port. But much of its historic fabric was lost to the plunder of successive English armies. The handsome 15th-century Dervorgilla Bridge has survived, as has the Midsteeple courthouse and prison (1707) on the High Street.

Among the many places devoted to the cult of Robbie Burns, who died in Dumfries in 1796, aged 37, is the Globe Inn (56 High Street), one of his favourite drinking haunts. Signposts lead to the Burns House on Burns Street, now a shrine to his memory, with manuscripts, letters and books— and the signature he obligingly scratched with his diamond ring on the bedroom window. He is entombed in a formidable Mausoleum at St Michael's Church, along with a statue of Robbie and the Muse. Housed in a water-mill out on Mill Road is the Robert Burns Centre, devoted to his last years in Dumfries.

Sweetheart Abbey
About 12 km (7 miles) due south of Dumfries, the lovely red sandstone ruin of Sweetheart Abbey was built by Cistercian monks in 1273. The grandiose Gothic edifice is so named because of the compulsive marital devotion of its patron, Lady Dervorgilla. She embalmed the heart of her dead husband Sir John Balliol (founder of Balliol College, Oxford) and carried it until her death 16 years later, when she was buried, with the heart, in the presbytery of the abbey-church.

Sweetheart: the last and most romantic of Scotland's Cistercian abbeys.

Caerlaverock Castle

The double-moated castle ruin, 13 km (8 miles) southeast of Dumfries, is beautifully located amid willow woods and marshland on the east bank of the Nith estuary as it flows into the Solway Firth. The castle was built to a unique triangular plan in the 13th century and was many times attacked and rebuilt over the next 300 years, resulting in the present combination of feudal crenellated towers and more graceful Renaissance façades. The nearby Caerlaverock Wildfowl and Wetlands Centre, covering 950 ha of salt marsh and mudflats, is famous for its wild whooper swans and barnacle geese.

Castle Douglas and Threave Garden

On Caerlingwalk Loch, almost midway between Dumfries and Kirkcudbright, Castle Douglas is in fact a town, laid out by Sir William Douglas in the 18th century. Nearby on the lochside road, Threave Garden attracts visitors to its rose and rhododendron gardens and the great springtime spectacle of daffodils—200 varieties. The garden is run by the National Trust for Scotland as a School of Horticulture.

Kirkcudbright

The town was built around the long-gone Kirk of Cuthbert, on an inlet of the Solway Firth. In the shadow of the towering mass of the 16th-century MacLellan's Castle, more mansion than fortress, an atmosphere of peace and mellow dignity reigns around the harbour. The town centre is a colourful mix of humble brick cottages, handsome Georgian villas and Victorian town houses that attracted leading painters known as the "Glasgow Boys". Among them, Edward Hornel made his home in the Georgian Broughton House on the High Street and designed its Japanese garden to go with his paintings of Japan, displayed here along with other works of the Glasgow school. Their paintings are also exhibited in the Tollbooth Art Centre, housed in what was once the town hall, court house and prison.

Galloway Forest Park

Britain's largest forest park covers over 750 sq km (300 sq miles) of pine-wooded hills, dramatic ravines, moorland, waterfalls and smooth lochs, with plentiful opportunities for the casual rambler or the dedicated long-distance hiker. On the park's southeast corner, the Visitors Centre at Clatteringshaw Loch is a good place to pick up trail maps and guides to the forest's flora and fauna. Wild goat, red deer, falcons and golden eagles can all be seen here. Explore the Rhinns of

Kells and Mullwarcher hills or take the easier 22-km (13-mile) footpath around the loch. It leads past Bruce's Stone, one of many places Robert the Bruce is said to have rested after one of his victories over the dastardly English.

Ayr

With its long sandy beach, the seaside town has retained all the airs of a Victorian resort still popular with the Glasgow gentry. Perhaps drawn by Burns's assurance that no other town surpasses it for "honest men and bonnie lasses", people continue to flock to the town's famous racecourse, founded in 1770. Although the town has a history dating back to the early 13th century, most of the medieval buildings have been demolished, and the neoclassical town hall with its imposing spire dates from the 19th century. Only the venerable cobbled Auld Brig was saved, celebrated in Burns's poetic homage to the 13th-century bridge spanning the River Ayr, which has been carefully restored. East of the bridge, paid for by Oliver Cromwell in 1654, the Auld Kirk has a noteworthy stone pulpit in its otherwise sombre interior. Loudon Hall (1534) on South Harbour Street is one of Scotland's oldest merchant houses. The *Waverley*, said to be the world's last sea-going paddle steamer, offers cruises from Ayr's harbour Monday to Wednesday and from Glasgow Harbour at the weekend.

The beach is southwest of the city centre, bordered by a long Esplanade with genteel Victorian villas and guesthouses, most of the latter around Wellington Square.

Alloway

Surrounded by Ayr's southern suburbs, this village is strictly for Burns buffs. Robbie was born here in 1759 and the whitewashed thatched Burns Cottage and Museum is the place he called his "auld cley biggin". The house, where he spent his first seven years, has original manuscripts, paintings and other personal possessions.

HIGHLIGHTS

- **Dumfries**: Memories of poet Robbie Burns
- **Kirkcudbright**: charming haven of peace for the "Glasgow Boys"
- **Galloway Forest Park**: ramblers head for pinewoods, mountains and lochs

CENTRAL SCOTLAND

Stirling and Surroundings, The Trossachs, Culross,
East Neuk of Fife, St Andrews, Perth

The famous wild landscape of Scotland—lochs and mountains, glens and forests—begins north of Glasgow and Edinburgh beyond the Firth of Forth. The great swathe of rolling countryside stretches from Loch Lomond in the east through the densely wooded hills and valleys of the Trossachs—where sits historic Stirling, its castle and battlefields —to the ancient kingdom of Fife and the North Sea coast, and the grand university town of St Andrews, royal home of the game of golf. Just north of Fife is Perth, and the historic palace of Scone.

Stirling and Surroundings

Its strategic location right in the centre of the country, bridging the River Forth amid otherwise impracticable marshy terrain, made Stirling the natural crossing point for armies negotiating a route between the north and south of Scotland. For this reason it attracted battles galore, not least the momentous Scottish victories over the English at Stirling Bridge in 1297 and nearby Ban-

Ancient and perhaps enchanted forest near Perth.

nockburn in 1314. The royal castle is Stirling's magnificent centrepiece, but there is much else to enjoy in the town, with its lively university population and pleasant shops, pubs and restaurants.

Stirling Castle

Dominating the town from its crowning height, the fortress can justly claim to be every bit as majestic as Edinburgh Castle. Its elongated crag, the 75-m (246-ft) high volcanic "plug" of igneous rock on which it is built, has served as a fortified position since the Picts controlled the region in pre-Roman times. The present castle dates largely from the 15th and 16th centuries, when it was a favoured residence of the Stuart monarchs.

Start your tour at the beautifully restored lime-washed sandstone Great Hall built by James IV in 1504. Among many spectacular banquets held here was one in December 1566 to celebrate the baptism of James VI (and future James I of England). This vast and lofty hall, 43 m (141 ft) long and 14 m (46 ft) wide, is the largest in Scotland, much larger than Edinburgh's— witness the five huge fireplaces needed to heat it. Behind the

Great Hall are the old Royal Kitchens. Long buried beneath the Grand Battery of cannons on the east curtain wall, they have been excavated to reveal how those banquets were prepared. They are peopled with life-size figures.

Directly opposite the Great Hall, the King's Old Building (1496) clings to the crag's highest point, the site of earlier castle keeps resisting western attackers. Appropriately, it is now a museum for the great regiment of Argyll and Sutherland Highlanders.

Between the two buildings, the handsome Chapel Royal was rebuilt in 1594 for the baptism of James VI's son Prince Henry.

On the north side of the courtyard (or Inner Close), James V's splendid Renaissance Palace was completed after his death in 1542. The voluptuous stone carving and graceful windows of the distinctly French façade were done by architects and masons of the king's widow Marie de Guise.

Town Wall

A fortified defence of massive basalt boulders was built in 1547 to protect the young Mary Queen of Scots from Henry VIII. The wall ran around the old town's southern perimeter. It can still be seen where it encircles the castle to the north along what is now the Back Walk, a scenic path that starts out from the tourist office on Dumbarton Road.

Old Town

Dating from the 12th century, the town of Stirling sprang up along cobbled streets south of the castle, and has grown ever since.

Immediately downhill from the castle, Argyll's Lodging is a fine example of a 17th-century town house, once the home of the Earl of Argyll. Below this is the imposing ruin of Mar's Wark, a never-completed 16th-century palace gutted in the Jacobite Rebellion of 1745.

Turn southeast onto Broad Street, once Stirling's market place, where the nicely restored buildings evoke the atmosphere of the medieval town.

Church of the Holy Rude

After a devastating fire, this splendid Gothic church of the Holy Rude (same as Holyrood, or Cross) was rebuilt in the 15th century; the choir and monumental apse were completed in 1555. The one-year-old King James VI (and future James I of England) was crowned here in 1567 after the forced abdication of his mother Mary Queen of Scots. Notice the remarkable 600-year-old oak-beamed roof of the nave, held together entirely by oak pegs.

Old Town Jail

On St John Street, this fearsome fortress was built in 1847 to replace the even worse, overcrowded 18th-century Tollbooth just across the street. It has been refurbished, with actors playing out the rigours of Victorian prison life. A little more refreshing is the rooftop view over the town to the Forth Valley.

Stirling's Bridges

North of the castle, a short distance downstream from the 15th-century Old Bridge, excavations have been carried out at the site of the original wooden Stirling Bridge where William Wallace scored his famous victory in 1297. Only a few foundations remain, at the bottom of the River Forth.

Wallace Monument

The tower honouring one of Scotland's most beloved military heroes was built in 1869 on the Abbey Craig hilltop 3 km (2 miles) north of Stirling. It was here that William Wallace stood in 1297, watching the advance of the English army towards Stirling Bridge. A climb of 246 steps leads to a magnificent view from a height of 67 m (220 ft) west to Ben Lomond and east to the old kingdom of Fife. On the way up, you can stop off to hear a talking statue of Wallace explaining his battle plans—with a much more convincing Scottish accent than Mel "Braveheart" Gibson—and see what is purported to be his original sword, 163 cm (64 inches) long.

Cambuskenneth Abbey

A short walk east of Stirling or, more picturesquely, down through a woodland path south of the Wallace Monument, the abbey's 14th-century belltower survives from an Augustinian monastery founded in 1147 by David I. Robert the Bruce held a parlia-

HIGHLIGHTS

- **Stirling Castle**: spectacular hilltop rival to Edinburgh Castle
- **Loch Lomond**: lake cruise to see the bonnie banks and bonnie braes in Scotland's newest national park
- **Culross**: beautifully restored 17th-century town
- **St Andrews**: cathedral, university and Royal & Ancient Golf Club
- **Scone Palace**: historic home of Scotland's monarchy

ment here in 1326, and it is the burial place of King James III (1451–88) and his wife Margaret.

Bannockburn

History buffs and Scottish patriots make the pilgrimage to the battlefield of Scotland's greatest military triumph over the English, on Midsummer's Day, 1314. A modern equestrian statue of victorious Robert the Bruce marks the spot, 3 km (2 miles) southeast of Stirling, and a Bannockburn Heritage Centre tells the battle's story. You can imagine the English army, outnumbering the Scots by three to one

but stuck in the marshy terrain between the Bannock Burn (stream) and the River Forth. Unable to manoeuvre their cavalry, they were slaughtered by Scottish pikemen attacking from their hill.

The Trossachs

Starting 20 km (12 miles) northwest of Stirling and extending to Loch Lomond, this is the stuff that many people's dreams of Scotland are made of. Mists and lonely blue mountains, silvery lochs and deep green forested glens turning gold and scarlet in autumn—they are all here. All it took was for Sir Walter Scott to sing of them in his *Lady of the Lake* in 1810 and the people began to flock here, Queen Victoria not the least among them. At high season, the tourists come in their thousands, but what some have called the "Highlands in miniature" are big enough to absorb all of them on walks in the mountains and in the depths of Queen Elizabeth Forest Park.

Callander

A 20-minute drive from Stirling, the village stands on the River Teith with Ben Ledi mountain looming to the west. Callander is the eastern gateway to the Trossachs, welcoming visitors with its antique galleries, Scottish woollen and craft shops, second-hand bookshops, quaint tea rooms and

---

OFF THE BEATEN TRACK

The Trossachs are extremely popular, but many escape the madding crowds by coming in the quieter days of spring and autumn. They can follow the trail of Sir Walter Scott's stag fleeing the hunter in the First Canto of *The Lady of the Lake*:

"The wily quarry shunned the shock,
And turned him from the opposing rock;
Then, dashing down a darksome glen,
Soon lost to hound and Hunter's ken,
In the deep Trossachs' wildest nook
His solitary refuge took."

restaurants. The tourist information centre is allied to the Rob Roy and Trossachs Visitor Centre in a converted church just off Main Street on Ancaster Square. Here, visitors can pick up information on the "Rob Roy Way", a 126-km (78-mile) hiking route along the highways and byways of the hero's adventures, between Drymen, south of Aberfoyle, and Pitlochry on the southern border of the Highlands.

Around Callander

While treks to the summit of Ben Ledi ("Mountain of God"), alt. 879 m (2,884 ft), may be for seasoned hikers only, Callander offers two other easier rambles in the hills behind the town. To the northeast, an hour's walk on a woodland trail takes you to and from Bracklinn Falls, a beautiful 15-m (47-ft) cascade that Scott called "Bracklinn's thundering wave". To the northwest, off the main A84 highway, a wooded gorge leads to the Falls of Leny.

Aberfoyle

This pretty village straddling the River Forth is an alternative to Callander as gateway to the Trossachs for visitors driving up from Glasgow rather than Stirling. Its slate quarries northwest of the town, now closed, were an important source of income in the 20th century. The slate was used most notably for the billiard tables on the *Queen Mary* luxury ocean liner. Today, Aberfoyle is a most hospitable base from which to explore the countryside on either side of its old stone bridge—north to Loch Achray and Loch Katrine or west to Loch Ard.

Lake Menteith

For some obscure linguistic reason, Menteith is Scotland's one lake rather than loch, a short drive east of Aberfoyle. Its well-stocked waters offer great fly-fishing for rainbow and brown

---

ROB ROY (1671–1734)

The Trossachs were the stamping ground of a bandit whom Walter Scott's novel and Hollywood's movies turned into a lovable Robin-Hood-style myth. Born in Glengyle at the northwest end of Loch Katrine, the real-life red-haired "Ruad Rob" ("Red Rob", anglicized to Rob Roy) stole cattle, enforced a brutal protection-racket on poor herders and farmers, and showed no political loyalties in plundering both sides indiscriminately during the Jacobite rebellion of 1715. He ended his days in peaceful piety in Balqhidder (northwest of Callander) where he is buried in the churchyard.

LOCHS AND LAKES

Asked the difference between a loch and lake, a Scottish girl in the Trossachs town of Aberfoyle replied: "A lake may be OK, but a loch is always a thing of beauty. It's likely to stretch out forever, be surrounded by wonderful forests and mountains, attract great heroes, poets and lovers, it's... it's... it's... oh, a loch's in Scotland and a lake isn't."

trout. On an island out in the middle, the 13th-century Inchmahome Priory stands in romantic roofless ruin surrounded by chestnut, ash and oak trees. The fugitive 5-year-old Mary Queen of Scots was concealed in the Augustine abbey on her way to France. In the church choir is the joint tomb of the Earl of Menteith and his wife Mary, reclining in tender embrace. Cunninghame Graham, a Scottish nationalist whose adventures in South America inspired his novelist friend Joseph Conrad's masterpiece *Nostromo*, was buried here in 1936.

Queen Elizabeth Forest Park
Established in 1953 to celebrate the coronation of Queen Elizabeth II, the park covers 16,780 ha of moorland and woodland from Loch Venachar to Loch Lomond.

It includes the headwaters of the River Forth on the eastern slopes of Ben Lomond. The Visitor Centre along Dukes Pass just north of Aberfoyle provides trail maps and information of the park's flora and fauna. Red and roe deer roam the park's ancient hunting forests of Achray and Loch Ard, while wild goat can be spotted on the mountain. Birdwatchers look out for greylag and merganser geese, teal duck and capercaillie, Scotland's biggest grouse.

Loch Lomond
This is the one with the "bonnie, bonnie banks", a beauty unspoiled by all the weekend pleasure-boats and day-trippers—Glasgow is just 30 km (18 miles) away. Formed by glaciers in the Ice Age, Britain's largest stretch of fresh water covers 71 sq km (28 sq miles), is 38 km (23 miles) long and up to 8 km (5 miles) wide, narrowing sharply to the north. Traffic along the western shore is busy, but it is worth stopping for the superb views from pretty villages like Luss and Tarbet across to the densely wooded eastern shore. The lake cruises start out from Balloch at the southern end of Lomond and cruise around some of the loch's 37 little islands. (The famous *Maid of the Loch* paddle steamer has undergone extensive refitting

and is open as a restaurant, with a registrar's license to perform civil weddings.)

Where the loch crosses the geological faultline of Scotland's highlands—through Balmaha on the eastern shore—the terrain grows noticeably more rugged in the shadow of Ben Lomond, alt. 974 m (3,195 ft) on the eastern shore. People taking the hikers', rather than the more strenuous climbers' route up the mountain, start out from the lochside car park at Rowardennan, an 11-km (6-mile) round trip with 940 m (3,084 ft) of climb.

Culross

East of Stirling on the north shore of the Firth of Forth, the white-washed and ochre houses of Culross (say "Coo-ross") take visit-ors back to the 17th century. Thanks to meticulous restoration by the National Trust for Scotland since the 1930s, the town's immaculate serenity makes a startling contrast with the gigantic Longannet power station and derelict Low Valleyfield colliery on either side and the Grangemouth oil refineries on the opposite shore. Yet Culross, too, was once an industrial town whose coal mines made a fortune for its entrepreneurial laird, Sir George Bruce. In 1588, James VI granted Culross the fiscally useful status of Royal Burgh in exchange for a piece of George Bruce's profits. The coal mines have gone, but the laird's handsome palace or Great Lodging still stands, now a largely 17th-century step-gabled ochre mansion at the western

HIGH AND LOW

Loch Lomond's famous song is supposedly sung by one of Bonnie Prince Charlie's soldiers captured in Carlisle during the rebellion of 1745. The love-lorn singer is to be executed and only his spirit will return to Scotland, by the "low road". His fellow soldier is to be released, but his "high road" over the rough hill country back to Scotland will take longer.

"By yon bonnie banks and by yon bonnie braes,
Where the sun shines bright on Loch Lomond.
Where me and my true love were ever wont to gae
On the bonnie, bonnie banks o' Loch Lomond.
"O ye'll tak' the high road and I'll tak' the low road,
An' I'll be in Scotland afore ye;
But me and my true love will never meet again
On the bonnie, bonnie banks o' Loch Lomond."

entrance to Culross. Its hall, parlours and chambers have beautiful pinewood panelling, one of them with allegorical paintings on its vaulted ceiling. The chequerboard medieval garden at the back is planted with vegetables typical of the period—skirret, kail and salsify—with mugwort and madder among its herbs.

In the city centre, the Culross story is nicely told in the Town House of the NTS headquarters, a historic building with ground-floor debtors' prison (manacles still embedded in the wall) and a cell up in the attic for "witches" awaiting execution in Edinburgh. At the east end of town, the 13th-century Cistercian Abbey lies in ruins—its monks were the town's first coal miners.

East Neuk of Fife
Known as a kingdom since the ancient Picts ruled there, Fife has maintained roughly the same area for over 1,600 years. It is bordered on three sides by water: the Firth of Forth to the south, Firth of Tay to the north and the North Sea to the east. The East Neuk, or corner, is a coastal stretch dotted with fishing villages and seaside resorts. Crow-stepped gables and roofs with curved pantiles give the houses a distinctly Dutch look, reflecting historic trade ties across the North Sea with the Netherlands.

Earlsferry and Elie
The two resorts, Earlsferry to the west and Elie to the east, share a bay with a fine sandy beach and rocky points at either end. Earlsferry is said to have acquired its name by providing the vessel by which Macduff, Earl of Fife, escaped from King Macbeth in 1054. Today, the harbour attracts more yachts than ferries. The most attractive old houses line South Street along the seafront. Behind this promenade, Earlsferry has the town hall while Elie has most of the village shops and the 17th-century parish church.

Pittenweem
Most of the East Neuk's fishing fleet make their home here, and the harbourside fish market bustles with activity from 8 a.m. Many of the Dutch-style gabled houses and inns, well restored, date back to the 17th century.

Anstruther
If Pittenweem has the fishing fleet, Anstruther has the fish and chips. The East Neuk's biggest village is seriously renowned for the most delicious fish'n'chips in Fife, in Scotland or in the world, according to whoever's talking. In a group of old houses overlooking the harbour, the Scottish Fisheries Museum traces the story of the national industry with a reconstructed boatyard, herring

One of Pittenweem's colourful fleet, heading out to sea.

market, a fisherman's cottage and models of boats throughout the ages. Harbour cruises go out to the Isle of May, a haven for thousand of puffin and eider duck. Its cliffs are breeding grounds for guillemots, kittiwakes and razorbills.

Crail

No other word for it, the fishing village of Crail is quaint. Beneath their rose-tinted pantiled or grey slate roofs, the houses make a colourful mixture of dazzling whitewash or russet and amber as they spill down to the honey-coloured stone walls of the harbour. The speciality here, as a weathered old sign proclaims, is not fish and chips but "lobster and dressed crab cooked while you wait". The broad Marketgate is the town centre, with the Dutch-looking town hall adjoining the old 16th-century Tollbooth at one end and St Mary's Church at the far end. Crail Museum and Heritage Centre (and tourist office) is at 62 Marketgate.

St Andrews

"Royal and Ancient". The name of the world's most famous golf club could just as well describe the town of St Andrews itself. The elegant east coast town traces its ancient beginnings to AD 732 57

The Old Course of the Royal and Ancient Golf Club, one of the world's most famous greens.

when monks founded the abbey whose church became St Andrews Cathedral. The town is also the home of Scotland's most ancient university. The medieval town-plan has remained—three main roads, North Street, Market Street and South Street leading to the cathedral and beyond that, to the harbour at the eastern edge of town.

The Cathedral

On a rocky windswept promontory above the harbour, a noble Gothic ruin is all that is left of the cathedral which, when consecrated in 1318 in the presence of Robert the Bruce, was the biggest church ever built in Scotland. After centuries of damage by fire, tempest and English armies, the *coup de grâce* was delivered in 1559 by plundering Reformation zealots spurred on by John Knox preaching in St Andrews parish church.

Of its fragmentary remains, much of the grand precinct wall still stands and a portion of the western façade. Beyond that, the grass-covered nave leads to a stone slab of the high altar where the relics of St Andrew were kept, and behind that, the monumental east window. St Rule's Tower, from an earlier abbey church, stands on the south side.

58

Medieval sculpture and other relics found on the site are displayed in the museum.

Southwest of the cathedral precincts are the Gothic vaults of the 14th-century Pends Gate, the old entrance to the priory on the road now leading down to the harbour.

The Castle
St Andrews' bishops lived here in relative safety, protected on three sides by sea and cliffs, with a moat on the landward side, until their fortress was devastated by religious warfare, falling into its present ruin in the 17th century. The splendid Visitors Centre in the castle's Foretower tells evenhandedly of the bloody murders of Protestant preachers and Catholic bishops. If you don't suffer from claustrophobia, take a guided visit of the "bottle dungeon" and the shafts of the siege mine and counter-mines.

The University
Founded in 1413 by James I for his tutor Bishop Henry Wardlaw, the university grew up around three colleges: St Salvator's (1450) with its college chapel still standing on North Street; St Leonard's (1511) on Pends Road (now a private girls' school); and St Mary's (1538) on South Street—its original building, with a beautiful grassy quadrangle, housing the Divinity Faculty.

PATRON SAINT
Andrew, patron saint of Scotland (and Russia), introduced his brother Simon (Peter) to Jesus and is regarded in many traditions as the first Apostle. He was crucified by the Romans at Patras, and, to avoid comparison with Jesus, is said to have asked that his cross be X-shaped (saltire)—as it appears on the Scottish national flag. Monks brought some of his bones from Patras, Greece, probably in the 8th century, to found the east coast settlement that grew into St Andrews.

The Royal and Ancient Golf Club
On the west side of town, these most hallowed of fairways, roughs, bunkers and greens are the object of golfing pilgrims from all over the world. There are six courses here, all public, but those who get to play the Old Course, with its 14 par 4s, two par 3s and two par 5s, will tell you they are now ready to die and go to heaven. The "R&A" is so holy in the eyes of the faithful that its coat of arms can blithely form St Andrew's X-shaped emblem from two crossed golfirons and nobody would dream of calling it sacrilege—"Andy would be honoured," says a pro at the Golf Shop. 59

On nearby Bruce Embankment, the excellent British Golf Museum tells the game's colourful story with computer screens and the truly ancient paraphernalia of clubs, balls, clothes, photos and film of all the greats.

Falkland Palace

A favourite haunt of the Stuart kings and queens, Falkland Palace and its beautifully landscaped gardens have regained the majesty of their 16th-century heyday. It was then that James IV and his son James V turned the 12th-century castle of the Macduffs, Earls of Fife, into a palatial hunting lodge for their deer and wild boar hunts in the surrounding forests. Its original Royal Tennis Court, the oldest in Britain still in use, was built in 1539. With their fanciful pepperpot towers, the present buildings are an attractive neo-Renaissance reconstruction of the 19th century. Best preserved are the Chapel Royal, the gallery of 17th-century Flemish tapestries and the King's Bedchamber, in which James V died on hearing, it is said, that his wife had given birth not to a son, but to a daughter, the future Mary Queen of Scots.

The pleasant country town also has several nicely restored 17th- and 18th-century houses and is popular as a base for walks in the Lomond hills.

Perth

Important for its inland harbour, the ancient town of Perth stands at the foot of the Grampian mountains on the west bank of

---

TEE TIME

Golf must have started in Scotland at least by the 1400s, because in 1457 James II tried to ban the game as it was diverting able-bodied men from the archery practice that was so much more important to homeland security. It is suggested the name comes from the Dutch word *kolf*, describing the club used to hit the ball, but nobody seriously suggests anybody but the Scots invented the actual game. Women made their appearance very early on when Mary Queen of Scots and her ladies-in-waiting were reprimanded for playing golf only a few days after the death of her husband Lord Darnley in 1567.

Leith claims to have opened the first links in the 15th century, but the British Golf Museum credits Perth with the first official course, in 1502, St Andrews coming only 50 years later. The R&A was founded in 1834, under the patronage of King William IV.

the River Tay, near where the Romans built a fort named Berta in AD 83. David I had a new town laid out in a gridplan in 1125. That compact city centre remains between two historic greens—the North Inch, where the Battle of the Clans was fought in 1396, and South Inch, used for political meetings and witch-burnings in the 17th century. These are now delightful public parks, thanks to the newly remodelled riverside at last fending off the frequently flooding Tay.

The 15th-century St John's Kirk, restored in the 1920s as a war memorial chapel, was the scene of a rabble-rousing sermon by John Knox in 1559 leading to the destruction of four monasteries. On the site of one of them on North Port, the Fair Maid's House is a picturesque cottage where Sir Walter Scott set his novel, *The Fair Maid of Perth*. Housed in the Round House on Marshall Place, the Fergusson Gallery presents the work of John Duncan Fergusson (1874–1961), a leading light of the Colourists working in Edinburgh and Paris.

Scone Palace

North of Perth and now the seat of the Earl of Mansfield, Scone (say "Scoon") Palace is a noble home, but a very much lived-in and even cosy residence. It was in the palace's abbey-church that Ken-

CLASH OF THE CLANS

North Inch is famous for the Battle of the Clans in 1396, when Robert III sought to end a Highland feud by staging a fight to the death between the Kays and Chattans. Thirty men from each clan fought in front of spectators including the royal court on specially built stands. Each man fired three bolts from his crossbow, and survivors then finished each other off with daggers and axes. At the end, 11 Chattans were still standing when the last Kay escaped by swimming across the Tay.

neth MacAlpin, lord of Kintyre, was crowned king on the Stone of Scone in 843. Both church and Stone have gone, but the palace has been restored around its 16th-century core, along with many of the medieval buildings that once received Macbeth and Robert the Bruce. The apartments display a magnificent porcelain collection and period furniture, including what is said to be Marie-Antoinette's writing desk. The chapel on Moot Hill is a neat little neo-Gothic affair, and the gardens are shared by peacocks and Highland cattle, with splendid groves of pine, Douglas fir (named after a 19th-century Scone gardener) and majestic oaks.

The sparsely populated region of Argyll extends west of Loch Lomond and its mountains to the coast, and north from the peninsula of Kintyre to the port of Oban. Argyll's Gaelic name defines the "coastland of the Gaels" settled by Irish Celts in the 5th century; the language is still spoken in rural communities. The notoriously erratic west coast weather has given the region some of Britain's finest gardens, notably around Inveraray, Tarbert and at Brodick Castle on Arran, the country's southernmost island, between the Kintyre peninsula and the Ayrshire coast.

Arran

Linked to the mainland by the ferry from Ardrossan to Brodick, the island is divided in two by the geological fault line between Scotland's Lowlands and Highlands. Mirroring the mainland, most of Arran's 4,500 population live in the gentler terrain of the south, with a climate noticeably milder than in the rugged mountain country of the north. Sportsmen can enjoy golf—seven courses around the island—and fishing, both deep sea off Brodick and Lamlash, and freshwater at Sliddery and Kilmory in the south or on Glen Sannox in the north.

Brodick

The island's capital is a bustling port town built around a bay with a grand mountain backdrop, topped by the Goatfell peak, alt. 874 m (2,867 ft). The Arran Heritage Museum presents the island's folklore in a crofter's converted 18th-century farm, but the town's major attraction is Brodick Castle. Since its 19th-century reconstruction, the former seat of the dukes of Hamilton is more stately home than castle, complete with 87 stag's heads on the staircase and a dazzling battery of copper in the huge Victorian kitchen. More interesting are the splendid gardens, boasting a great array of rhododendrons, and a country park with marked woodland trails around ponds, waterfalls and ravines.

Lamlash

With its bay sheltered by the little Holy Island, this genteel Victorian resort is popular for sailing of all sorts, yachting, deep-sea fishing (for mackerel, cod, plaice and flatfish), even serving as a naval anchorage in World War I. On the village green facing the bay, a

Fishing boats jostle with pleasure craft in the port of Tarbert.

simple monolith monument commemorates the forced emigration to Canada in 1829 of 11 Lamlash farming families, as part of Britain's brutal Clearance policy.

Holy Island is now a Buddhist retreat, but the public is welcome to ramble around its coast and up the slopes of Mullach Mor, alt. 314 m (1,030 ft), as long as they make no fires and do not bring dogs or alcohol.

Kildonan

The pretty little village at the southeast corner of Arran attracts people to one of its few sandy beaches, complete with a slightly rickety, ivy-covered castle ruin, looking out at the lighthouse on the offshore isle of Pladda.

At nearby Kilmory, the local Torrylinn Creamery produces a much admired tangy cheese known as Arran Dunlop.

Blackwaterfoot

On the west coast, this pleasant little village overlooks the pebble beaches of Drumnadoon Bay. Its Shiskine Golf Club claims the world's only 12-hole golf course —par 42, with fairways crossed by sudden sea-breezes and the occasional wild mink.

A brisk walk to the north brings you to the King's Cave, one among a dozen vying for the location of Robert the Bruce's encounter with the spider that taught him to try, try, try again, before finally defeating the English at Bannockburn.

Further north by road at Machrie Moor are neolithic stone circles tracing round-houses and burial cairns up to 5,500 years old.

Lochranza

Quite apart from being the ferry port linking Arran to the Kintyre peninsula, the village is worth a visit for its enchanting situation on the lagoon, Loch Ranza, from which it takes its name, surrounded on three sides by hills. The 13th-century castle stands in ruin on the lagoon's shingle flats. A more modern monument is the Isle of Arran Distillery, open only since 1995 and producing the first legal Arran Malt in 150 years.

Kintyre

On the Argyll mainland west of Arran, only a narrow neck of land at its northern end prevents the Kintyre peninsula from being an island. The charming little fishing village of Tarbert—Gaelic for

The story of Robert the Bruce and his spider was first written down, some say invented, in 1828 by—who else?—Sir Walter Scott in his *Tales of a Grandfather*. He said that as a result, Scots named Bruce would never harm a spider. It is indeed widely believed in Scotland that killing a spider brings bad luck, in particular making it rain. Any excuse will do.

"isthmus"—attracts many yachts and other pleasure boats to its inlet harbour, but most motorists take the Arran ferry from Lochranza across to Claonaig. Using the west coast highway, wild and windswept but faster than the single-track road on the east coast, many are making a pilgrimage to the lighthouse at Mull of Kintyre. The peninsula's desolate southwestern tip and Britain's closest point to Ireland, a mere 19 km (12 miles) away, is the object of a famous song by Paul McCartney. The chorus does mention a "mist rolling in from the sea" that may occasionally obstruct the view of Ireland.

Campbeltown

On the way south, the road passes through Kintyre's "capital". Of the 34 single-malt distilleries that once gave it its distinctive odour, only one is now active, but in the pubs, you can still hear the song, *Campbeltown Loch, I wish you were whisky*. The town's story is told in its Heritage Centre in the former Lorne Street church, but the architectural jewel is the Wee Picture House (1913), an authentic Art Deco cinema on Hall Street.

Inveraray

This delightful piece of 18th-century Georgian urban planning was built on a promontory on Loch Fyne's eastern shore by the Duke of Argyll. It replaced a crumbling fishing village razed to make way for his new castle.

Main Street is lined by two immaculate rows of whitewashed terraced houses with elegant black window frames. At the top of the street, the neoclassical All Saints Church was divided into a north half for English-speaking worshippers and a south half for Gaelic-speakers. The belltower added after World War I, with ten very loud bells, offers splendid rooftop views over Loch Fyne and the Argyll forests.

East of the church, Inveraray Jail houses an elegant Georgian courthouse and a museum recreating prison life from the Middle Ages to the present day.

Inveraray Castle, still home to the Dukes of Argyll, was built in

1746 just north of town, with French-style gables and pepper-pot towers. Surviving two big fires, it has some fine Gainsborough paintings, handsome furniture and a formidable display of armour and weaponry, including Rob Roy's dirk, the traditional Highland dagger.

Crarae Garden

A short drive southwest of Inveraray, Crarae Garden was laid out in the early 1900s in a spectacular ravine tumbling down to Loch Fyne. The gorgeous colours of hundreds of azaleas and rhododendrons are set against a backdrop of eucalyptus and soaring conifers.

Bonawe

Northwest of Inveraray and some 20 km (12 miles) from Oban, the Bonawe Iron Furnace is a fascinating industrial heritage site in what is now lovely parkland on the north side of the village of Taynault. It is operated by Historic Scotland, the agency that safeguards the nation's monuments, listed buildings and heritage sites.

From 1753 to 1876, England's iron manufacturers found it economical to transport iron ore from Furness in Cumbria to Bonawe to be smelted in its blast furnace, fuelled by the abundant charcoal supplies from Argyll forests. Rough pig iron was sent back down by rail to forges in England. Today, the smelting process is illustrated in Bonawe's iron ore sheds. About 4,000 ha (10,000 acres) of woodland were used to smelt the annual output of 700 tons of pig iron. The oak, birch, alder and hazel trees of nearby forests were not felled but coppiced, with branches lopped off in rotation. When charcoal was replaced by coke, smelting reverted to England, and Bonawe closed down.

Oban

With the advent of Victorian steamers and latter-day car ferries serving the Inner Hebrides and Western Isles, Oban has grown into the west coast's biggest port and by far the busiest. For those with a moment to spare before travelling on, a 10-minute uphill slog to the town's colossal landmark, McCaig's Folly, is a must. Banker John Stuart McCaig built this replica of Rome's Colosseum in 1897 to give work to unemployed stone-masons—and as a monument to himself and his family, though he never got round to erecting the planned statues. Inside is just a grassy hilltop, but great views of the town and its bay do reward the effort. Bay cruises and island tours start out from the harbour's North, South and Railway piers.

SKYE, INNER HEBRIDES AND WESTERN ISLES

Portree, Trotternish, Waternish, Cuillin Hills, Sleat, Isle of Mull, Iona, Islay, Western Isles

Once known collectively as the Hebrides, Inner and Outer, 40 islands and countless rocky islets curve in a great arc off the Atlantic coast of the northwest mainland. Buffeted by the winds and waves, only a few are inhabited, but Skye and the neighbouring Western Isles are popular both with mainstream tourists and hardier ramblers seeking to get off the beaten track among the islands' many spectacular mountains.

Skye, the most popular of Scotland's island destinations, the largest and northernmost of the Inner Hebrides, lives up to its romantic link with Bonnie Prince Charlie and the song associated with him. Its deeply indented coastline gives it a series of dramatic mountainous peninsulas, Trotternish and Waternish in the north, Sleat in the south, fertile and green with a couple of sandy beaches. Between them is Minginish and the grand jagged peaks of the Cuillin Hills, red to the west and black to the east. The fiercely feuding MacLeod and MacDonald clans left the island its share of medieval castles, many in ruins—and a strong Gaelic culture. Access to the island is easy: 30 minutes by ferry from Mallaig to Armadale in the southwest corner, or over the Skye Bridge from Kyle of Lochalsh to Kyleakin on the southeast coast. The main A87 highway leads north to Skye's main town of Portree, a good base from which to explore the wilder north.

Portree

From a Gaelic name meaning the King's Port, ever since it was used by James V in 1540, Portree is Skye's principal town, centring on a harbour with an attractive backdrop of tree-covered cliffs. The peninsula escarpment overlooking the harbour is known with characteristic island romanticism as The Lump, where Skye used to hang its criminals, a much appreciated public entertainment. The steamers from Glasgow and the Western Isles, and the fishing fleet that kept the port busy in the 19th century, have given way to pleasure craft and just a few remaining fishing vessels. The pier was the work of the great 19th-century Scottish engineer Thomas Telford, builder of

From Skye's Trotternish peninsula you can look out over the sea to the Highlands.

Skye's first important highways. Above the harbour, in the clean and tidy town centre, is the site of MacNab's Inn (now the Royal Hotel on Bank Street) where Bonnie Prince Charlie, hunted by government troops, said farewell to the lovely Flora Macdonald in 1746.

Trotternish

Some of Skye's most spectacular scenery is packed into the thumb-shaped peninsula extending north of Portree. Volcanic action over millions of years has literally packed the basalt rock into wonderful concertina-like cliffs or splintered it off into solitary giant needle outcrops on the narrow coastal plain.

Old Man of Storr

The east coast road runs from Portree past Loch Fada ("Long") and Loch Leathan ("Broad") to where the Storr mountain rises 719 m (2,360 ft) above the inland cliffs and the Old Man of Storr. The mountain seems to have thrown down this formidable column of rock, 50 m (164 ft) high, to challenge even the hardiest rock-climbers. Further north are two impressive waterfalls, both signposted, the Lealt Falls tumbling into a densely wooded ravine and the Mealt Falls hurling itself over the Kilt Rock cliffs, so named for the patterns of their vertical "pleats" and horizontal splits. Birdwatchers will spot plenty of kittiwakes and fulmars.

Staffin Bay
Staffin is the main town on this east coast. Its museum displays many of the fossils and dinosaur bones found in the sandy bay. Beyond the bay are the peninsula's most striking set of rock formations, the towering pinnacles of the Quiraing.

Duntulm Castle
The dramatic cliffs of Rubha Hunish mark the northern tip of the peninsula (good whale-spotting) with the ruins of Duntulm Castle to the south. The fortress was a redoubt of the MacDonald clan until 1732 when it was abandoned after a clumsy nurse dropped the chief's baby son from a window onto the rocks below.

Museum of Island Life
South down the west coast, Skye's Museum of Island Life is housed in an imposing group of black thatched cottages vividly recounting the crofters' work and living habits in the 19th century. In the hillside cemetery behind the museum are the graves and memorial of Flora MacDonald and her husband who died in nearby Kilmuir.

The ferry port of Uig, gateway to the Western Isles (Harris and Uist), has a good pottery shop and an excellent brewery.

Waternish
The narrow peninsula west of Trotternish is great hiking country for people wanting to escape the mob and enjoy romantic solitary views across to the Western Isles. From the A850 highway take the B886 north to Stein, a pretty village of whitewashed cottages with a splendid 16th-

HIGHLIGHTS
- **Trotternish Peninsula**: wild landscape of crazy rock formations
- **Cuillin Hills**: Skye's landmark scenery of red and black mountains
- **Islay Single-Malt Whisky Trail**: tasty tour of famous distilleries
- **Tobermory**: western Scotland's prettiest fishing port
- **Calanais Stones**: remarkable prehistoric standing stones
- **South Uist**: away from it all on Western Isles' best beaches

69

SKYE'S CATCH-22

In Trumpan graveyard stands a Trial Stone, a pillar with a hole in it. If an accused person, blindfolded, could find the hole without fumbling and put their hand through it, they were declared innocent. The odds were better than for the witches thrown into the loch: if they could swim, they were guilty and were burned to death; if they drowned, they were innocent.

century pub, the Stein Inn. At the northern end of the road, the clifftop medieval church of Trumpan lies in eloquent ruin since the dreadful fire of 1578 burned alive a whole congregation of MacLeods. This was in reprisal by the MacDonalds after hundreds of their kin had suffered a similar fate at the hands of the MacLeods a year earlier when taking refuge in a cave on the island of Eigg.

Dunvegan Castle

Just south of Waternish, the MacLeods' castle dates back to the 15th century but Victorian restoration gives it the classic Scottish baronial look. On show are several quasi-sacred relics: Rory Mor's Horn, a formidable drinking vessel that a new clan chief was obliged to empty of its claret at one draught, "without setting down or falling down"; the almost obligatory lock of Bonnie Prince Charlie's hair; and a silken Fairy Flag said to have been brought back from Constantinople with magical powers for the clan in battle. The most attractive feature of the visit is the castle gardens stretching down to the castle's loch.

Cuillin Hills

At the heart of the island, the serrated silhouette of the Cuillin peaks is Skye's most prominent landmark, providing an orientation point from each of the island's peninsulas. Dividing into two distinctive rock formations, the hills are a geologist's delight. To the west, the Black Cuillins take their name from the jagged peaks of dark grey, coarse-grained glabbro rock, while to the east the Red Cuillins' more rounded peaks are of russet-hued granite. Any casual rambler can enjoy the splendid landscapes of the Cuillins, but only the most experienced mountain-climbers attempt the 20 or so "Munros". These are peaks over 915 m (3000 ft) named after Hugh Thomas Munro, who listed Scotland's highest mountains in 1891.

Glen Sligachan

With its famous mountaineers' hotel, Sligachan is the gateway to the Cuillins for visitors using the A87 highway northwest from the Skye Bridge or south from Portree. Succeeding an inn that has been at the head of Loch Sligachan since the 1700s, the hotel provides guidance and sustenance for ramblers and climbers. Glen Sligachan cuts south through the hills, neatly dividing the tough Black Cuillins from the easier Red. The glen forks southeast through the narrow glacial Loch Coruisk with splendid views of the Cuillins' tallest peaks. South of the glen is the sandy bay of Camasunary.

Carbost

On the shore of Loch Harport, the village grew up around the Talisker Distillery, established in 1830 and Skye's only producer of single malt. Guided tours (and, naturally, tastings) take place every half-hour, all year round.

Glen Brittle

The fraternity of hardened climbers meet in this stony glen on the western edge of the Black Cuillins to tackle their most challenging peaks. From the beautifully situated village of Glen Brittle, with its sandy beach, there is

FLORA AND CHARLIE

Daughter of a tenant farmer, Flora MacDonald is an immortal heroine of Scottish history for having helped Bonnie Prince Charlie escape from the clutches of government redcoats. She was just 23 when she met the prince on the island of South Uist after his defeat at Culloden. With the bonnie fugitive disguised as an Irish maid named Betty Burke, she sailed "over the sea to Skye". They separated at Portree, he to continue on to France and a miserable alcoholic end and she, for her pains, to a cell in the Tower of London. Amnestied after a year, Flora married a fellow MacDonald and emigrated to North Carolina before finally settling back on Skye at Kingsburgh. It was Robert Louis Stevenson who wrote the haunting song:

Sing me a song of a lad that is gone,
Say, could that lad be I?
Merry of soul he sailed on a day
Over the sea to Skye.
Billow and breeze, islands and seas,
Mountains of rain and sun,
All that was good, all that was fair,
All that was me is gone

also a slightly easier 8-km (5-mile) round-trip to Coire Lagan to an ice-cold lochan (or little lake) and back. Towering above it is Skye's tallest peak, Sgurr Alasdair, at 993 m (3,258 ft).

Elgol

At the southern tip of the Strathaird peninsula, this ferry port provides some of the most spectacular views of the Cuillins, particularly on the approach road southwest from Broadford. The single-track B8083 passes the Kilchrist church ruin, a picturesque graveyard and old white marble quarries, and gives you a splendid view of the Blaven peak, 928 m (3,044 ft), beyond Loch Slapin. The scenic journey ends with the steep descent into Elgol, its houses hugging the hillside down to the jetty.

Sleat

Visitors coming in or out of Skye via the ferry port of Armadale might care to take a look at the island's green and fertile southern peninsula. The castle at Armadale, headquarters of the MacDonalds, is more interesting for its lovely gardens than the heavily restored castle itself.

Sleat's west coast has some nice sandy beaches at Tarskavaig, looking over to the isles of Rhum and Eigg, and at Ord, with a spectacular view north to the Cuillins.

Isle of Mull

Increasingly popular but still less crowded than Skye, this cheerful and hospitable island offers a wide variety of scenery: charming fishing villages in sheltered harbours give way to jagged craggy coastlines; pleasant, rolling green hills alternate with bleak moorland; and the mountainous interior culminates in the 966 m (3,169 ft) peak of Ben More. Ferries come into east coast ports: Craignure from Oban or Fishnish from Lochaline.

Torosay Castle

Immediately south of Craignure (a jolly little train ride by Mull Rail, if you wish), the castle has been rebuilt as a classical baronial pile with good Edwardian furnishings and Victorian paintings. But its main attraction, watched over by the statues of 18th-century Italian sculptor Antonio Bonazza, is its superb terrace and "niche" gardens extending over 5 ha down to the sea. A mild Gulf Stream climate provides a rich vegetation for the ornamental gardens peopled with statues, stone lions and a folly, and including the Japanese garden, the old rock garden and the Western Highland bog garden.

Tobermory

Lining the harbour on Main Street, gaily painted houses,

Tobermory is full of delights: colourful houses, a pretty harbour, a whisky distillery—and a chocolate makers!

shops, hotels and pubs rival the pinks, blues and yellows of the yachts and smaller vessels to make this quite the cheeriest fishing port along Scotland's west coast. Other houses, immaculately whitewashed, crown the wooded hillside behind the harbour. Efforts in the 18th century failed to make Tobermory a centre for herring fishery, but the island's capital happily settles for its present role as a thriving tourist centre—and setting for the children's TV programme *Balamory*. In a converted bakery on Main Street, Mull Museum tells the island's story, while the tiny Tobermory Distillery offers tours and tastings of its single-malt tipple. Some of it goes into the chocolates of the Tobermory Chocolate Company at the top of the town.

The tourist office has information about the island's wildlife expeditions to see otters, porpoises, golden eagles, white tailed sea eagles and hen harriers (marsh hawks). Whale-watching cruises are organized here by the Hebridean Whale and Dolphin Trust.

Dervaig

Through the delightful countryside of green meadows and blue lochs west of Tobermory, a sin- 73 gle-track road dives and twists uphill and down dale some 12 km (20 miles) to the pretty village of Dervaig. At the head of Loch a'Chumhainn, Dervaig's neat little whitewashed cottages are grouped in twos along the main street laid out in 1799. Kilmore Church is notable for its cylindrical steeple shaped like a finely sharpened pencil, but the town is best known for its Mull Theatre. Installed since 1966 in a converted coach house, it is said to be the smallest professional theatre in Britain, seating 43 and producing both avant-garde and family drama for regular tours to Edinburgh and Glasgow.

Calgary

West of Dervaig, this tiny village has the island's best beach, a broad stretch of fine white sand on Calgary Bay. To correct a commonly told story, the village's better-known Canadian namesake was not settled by local victims of the mid-century Clearances, but so named in 1876 by Lieutenant-Colonel James Macleod of the North West Mounted Police after visiting his cousins' ancestral estate on Calgary Bay.

Iona

Hugging the southwest tip of Mull, the small island attracts thousands of pilgrims every year to the site of the monastery founded in 563 by St Columba and 12 disciples. The Irish monk is credited with converting Scotland and much of northern England to Christianity. North of the port of Baile Mór, the present abbey was founded by Benedictines around 1200 and rebuilt in the 15th century. The 20th-century restoration does justice to the handsome Gothic cloisters and church, in particular the sculpted capitals preserved in the choir and the south transept. Nothing remains from Columba's era, but a shrine for his tomb stands to the left of the abbey entrance. The abbey cemetery and St Oran's Chapel were the burial place for successive Scottish kings up to Macbeth in 1057.

Staffa

This exquisite uninhabited isle is just a short boat trip west of Mull (ferries from Dervaig and the port of Ulva Ferry). Staffa, from the Norse for "pillars", is famous for its striking cliffs of black basalt polygonal organ pipes. The spectacular pillars around Fingal's Cave—what Wordsworth called "Fingal's mystic grot"—inspired Felix Mendelssohn's Hebrides overture (he made the trip in 1829), as well as a painting by Turner. Fingal—Finn MacCumhaill—was a legendary Celtic warrior. Cruises usually include the Tresnish Isles, northwest of

Staffa, including Lunga, a bird-watcher's favourite for its puffins, guillemots and razorbills.

Islay

Its position in the Gulf Stream gives the southernmost of the Inner Hebrides a relatively mild climate. Ferries from Kennacraig on Kintyre come into Port Ellen—with an airport further north for flights from Glasgow. Islay (pronounced *Eye-la*) attracts whisky connoisseurs to its seven single-malt distilleries and bird-watchers to the unspoiled lochs and marshland on the west side of the island. There is excellent golf at Machrie, north of Kintra.

Whisky Trail

Port Ellen is the gateway to the south coast's renowned single-malt whisky distilleries at Lava-gulin, Laphroaig and Ardbeg, each offering a tasting. Beautifully perched on a promontory east of Lagavulin is the ruin of 16th-century Dunyvaig Castle. East of Ardbeg is the 13th-century Kildalton Chapel. With a particularly good visitor's programme, the oldest of the distilleries is up at Bowmore, the island's capital and headquarters of the tourist office. Other distilleries are located on the northeast coast at Caol Ila and Bunnahabhain, and across the Lochindaal Bay from Bowmore at Bruichladdich. The very names seem to contain the peaty smoke of the tangy single malt.

Port Charlotte

Founded in 1828, this lovely village of spotless whitewashed cottages is a favoured base for exploring the island's wildlife, especially its birds. The excellent Islay Wildlife Centre provides guidance for nature-lovers. Bird-watchers looking for barnacle geese, red-breasted merganser and golden eagles head up to Loch Gorm and the Gruinart Flats or across the Rinns (hilly ridge) of Islay to Kilchiaran.

Western Isles

The remote and wilder islands forming a crescent west and north of Skye attract people who prefer to escape the latter's crowds. Exposed to the rough seas of the Atlantic, the sparsely populated islands, which are also known as the Outer Hebrides, have dramatically craggy shorelines with towering cliffs and just a few sheltered bays. In the interior, landscapes range from the bleak peat moors of Lewis in the north to the barren peaks of North Harris and more colourful heather-covered mountains of South Harris, sloping down to some fine sandy beaches. Further south, the islands of North and South Uist are marked by windswept sandy 75

Fingal's Cave on Staffa, formed entirely of hexagonal pillars of basalt.

beaches surrounding the interior's boggy farmland. The Western Isles' remoteness has sustained the Gaelic culture (and place names), with the austere Calvinist religion of the Free Church on the northern islands and the more relaxed Catholic faith in South Uist and the other smaller southern islands.

Lewis and Harris

These are in fact two parts of one island connected by a narrow isthmus at Tarbert. With a population of around 21,000, this is the largest of the Western Isles. Ferry and air passengers come in at the main town of Stornoway on the northeast coast—*Steornabhagh* in Gaelic. The grand Scottish baronial-style Town Hall on South Beach exhibits local artists in its An Lannair Art Gallery, on the first floor.

Aficionados of the famously robust Harris Tweed fabric (not actually made on Harris) can see it being produced at the Lewis Loom Centre on Cromwell Street, in a delightful old stone building, its beams made from old telegraph poles, ship's masts and driftwood.

Callanish (Calanais)

The village, west of Stornoway, has a series of Standing Stones, many of them between 4 m and 5 m (13–16 ft) high, erected 3000 and 4000 years ago. At the edge of Loch Roag, a sea loch forming an inlet on the northwest coast, the monoliths are arranged in circles linked by an avenue. Like gaunt, grey ghosts on the hillside, they are apparently aligned with significant points in the lunar cycle, perhaps for the use of Stone Age farmers. The usual New Age suspects like to speculate on extraterrestrial interpretations and human sacrifice. Local legend recounts that a "shining one" walks along the avenue at dawn on midsummer's day. There are three sets of Standing Stones, Calanais I, II and III, and a Visitor Centre with a small exhibition on a hillside south of the main site.

North Uist

The ferry port is at Lochmaddy (*Loch nam Madadh*). While here, take a look at the first-class museum and arts centre housed in the 18th-century merchant's house of Taigh Chearsabhagh.

Just outside Lochmaddy are the prehistoric sites of the hillside Barpa Langais burial cairn and the Pobull Fhinn stone circle at the edge of Loch Langais. Then, to really get away from it all, head for the great sandy beaches on the north and west coasts, both for bathing and bird-watching.

South Uist

The island can fairly lay claim to the best of the Western Isles' beaches, which run the whole length of the west coast. Howmore (*Tobha Mòr*), a beautiful village of thatched cottages, provides the best access to the shoreline of golden or silver-grey sands. These are backed by a landscape of *machair*—the grassy, lime-rich land characteristic of the coasts of Scotland's western Highlands.

About 8 km (5 miles) south of Tobha Mòr, the Kildanon Museum does a delightful job of illustrating life on South Uist from the Bronze Age to the present day. Immediately south of the museum is a cairn serving as a memorial to Flora MacDonald, whose childhood home was nearby.

St Kilda

Some 65 km (40 miles) west of the main Western Isles, the three little islands of St Kilda have been uninhabited since the 1930s and are now a nature reserve operated by the National Trust for Scotland.

Part of the main island of Hirta is a military radar-tracking station, but the rest of the archipelago constitutes a major seabird breeding centre—fulmars, puffins and the world's largest colony of gannets.

On its great triangle jutting out into the North Sea, Scotland's northeast region has two major urban centres, Dundee at the southern tip, an industrial stronghold of the 19th century, and newly oil-rich Aberdeen on the east coast. The region is known for its royal castles around the River Dee and its world-famous malt whisky distilleries around the River Spey. Rising above the two river valleys, the Grampian and Cairngorm mountains extend west and north to herald the Highlands.

Dundee

The town's 19th-century industrial grandeur has gone, but the town still enjoys a spirited cultural life, with some fine museums and a spectacular new building by world-renowned architect Frank Gehry. Something of Dundee's old urban vigour can be seen from the view of its skyline as you cross the Tay Road Bridge, 2,250 m (1.4 miles) long, with its pedestrian walkway along the centre (running parallel to the older Tay Rail Bridge). The city made its name and fortune on three J's—jam, jute and journalism. Keillers, the jam manufacturers, have moved elsewhere, but their most famous product continues under its original name of Dundee Orange Marmalade. As a supplement to linen production, jute made local textile manufacturers a tidy income until they succumbed to Calcutta's fierce competition in the 20th century. Journalism has survived and thrived with DC Thomson newspapers and, for many people, the even more important *Beano* and *Dandy* comics, still going strong.

City Centre

Large-scale restoration has spruced up the city centre around City Square, with its imposing Caird Hall doubling as a concert hall and conference centre. Even more imposing is the huge bronze statue nearby of stubble-bearded Desperate Dan, the mighty hero of *Dandy,* striding along the High Street with his "dawg". Albert Square is the home of DC Thomson's comics and newspapers, in the grand red sandstone Courier Building. Here, too, is Gilbert Scott's superb Victorian neo-Gothic building for the McManus Art Galleries and Museum. The collections are devoted to the

The small copper pot stills of Glenfiddich distillery.

city's history, musical instruments, the decorative arts, and European and Scottish paintings of the 19th and 20th centuries.

West Side

Many cultural facilities are located around the University of Dundee, west of the city centre. Imaginatively converted from a car showroom and garage, the splendid Dundee Contemporary Arts building at 152 Nethergate combines a print studio, art galleries, two art cinemas and a fashionable café contrasting with the surrounding industrial wasteland. Just north on Tay Square, the Dundee Rep Theatre is a vibrant home of modern and traditional drama and the Scottish Dance Theatre.

Further north on West Henderson Wynd, the fascinating Verdant Works is a disused jute mill converted into a museum telling the story of the jute industry, with demonstrations on machines once used for training new factory workers.

Maggie's Centre

On the west side of town at Ninewells Hospital, the ultra-modern Maggie's Centre is an outstanding design by Canadian-born Frank Gehry. Opened in September 2003, this support centre for cancer patients is the first to be constructed in Britain by the world-famous architect. With Gehry's trademark free-form roofs and distinctive white tower, it is one of Scotland's most important new buildings.

Discovery Point

Down by the Tay Road Bridge is the *RRS Discovery*, the steam-mechanized three-master built in Dundee in 1901 for British explorer Robert Scott's expeditions to the Antarctic, the last culminating in his death in 1911. It has been refurbished to tell the story of his fateful adventures.

Meigle Museum

In Meigle, a village some 24 km (16 miles) north of Dundee, the plain and simple schoolhouse

---

HIGHLIGHTS

- **Meigle**: Scotland's best museum of ancient Pictish Stones
- **Glamis Castle**: the late Queen Mum's childhood home with legendary ghosts left by Macbeth
- **Balmoral**: Queen Victoria's bequest to the Royal Family and their fans
- **Malt Whisky Trail**: high spirits on beautiful Speyside

provides a museum for Scotland's finest collection of Pictish and early-Christian stones, 26 on display dating between the 7th and 10th centuries. These tombstones and monumental crosses are variously inscribed with human and animal figures and ritual symbols of often largely obscure significance. One of them was discovered in the masonry of an abandoned whisky distillery. The most remarkable is a slab 2.5 m (8 ft) tall with a cross on one side and on the other, equestrian figures, a centaur and dragon and what is believed to be a depiction of the Biblical Daniel in the lions' den.

Glamis Castle

Due north of Dundee against a dramatic backdrop of the Grampian Mountains, Glamis Castle is associated in legend with Shakespeare's *Macbeth* and in modern history as the childhood home of Elizabeth Bowes Lyon, the late Queen Mother, and the birthplace of Princess Margaret. It was built in the 11th century as a modest hunting lodge and remodelled in the 17th century as the castle of today, with its veritable forest of towers, pepperpot turrets and statues. It is reputed to have at least nine resident ghosts. Pronounced *glahmz*, the castle was the family home of the Earls of Strathmore, the 14th being the father of Elizabeth Bowes Lyon, who married England's future George VI. The guided tour takes in the Dining Room, Great Hall, family Chapel (1688), the 15th-century Crypt and the so-called Duncan's Hall, imagined setting for the Scottish king's murder by Shakespeare's Macbeth (historians suggest he actually died in battle near Elgin). Of the castle's many Flemish paintings, the best is Frans Snyder's *Fruit Market* in the Billiard Room. The landscaped gardens have grand avenues of beeches and woodlands of majestic Douglas firs.

Aberdeen

Scotland's third-largest city (pop. 203,000) grew up where the River Don and River Dee flow into the North Sea. Historically prosperous as a trading port and in the 19th century from the fishing and shipbuilding industries, the city revived its fortunes in the 1970s with the development of North Sea oil. It has 130 offshore oil platforms. Granite quarried in the nearby Grampian mountains has provided the raw material for the city's major monuments, a lucrative resource for overseas trade—giving Aberdeen its nickname of Granite City.

Around Union Street

Union Street, the main thoroughfare, slopes down through the city 81

The centre of social life in every town and village, pubs have become the Scots' most popular places for eating out.

centre to Castlegate at its east end. The castle has gone, but the cobbled market square is still marked by the 17th-century Mercat Cross, a hexagonal base decorated with gargoyles and carvings of Scottish kings, supporting a post topped by a white unicorn.

On Union Street itself, the medieval Tollbooth in the granite Town Hall was once a prison and now serves as a museum of the ignoble arts of incarceration.

Just off Broad Street, Provost Skene's House (1545), 45 Guestrow is Aberdeen's oldest surviving private house, now displaying the lifestyle of a wealthy 17th-century merchant.

Marischal College

On Broad Street, the towering neo-Gothic college, Britain's largest granite building, houses a fine Anthropological Museum. Exhibits include Egyptian antiquities, a canoe from Papua New Guinea, a Tibetan prayer wheel, Inuit (Eskimo) carvings and an "Encylopaedia of the Northeast" tracing the story of the Aberdeen region from Pictish carvings to modern whisky distilling.

Art Gallery

With its façade of Corinthian columns, the neoclassical gallery on Schoolhill provides an elegant home for the city's major collection of Scottish and British artists (Raeburn, McTaggart, Ramsay and Reynolds); French painters (Courbet, Monet, Pissarro, Renoir and Bonnard); and 20th-century artists (Francis Bacon, Ben Nicholson and sculptor Barbara Hepworth).

Union Terrace Gardens

Escape the city bustle in the sunken gardens west of the Art Gallery, with their summer brass-band concerts and a fine view across to the three domed buildings of the Central Library, St Mark's Church and His Majesty's Theatre, known collectively to Aberdonians as "Education, Salvation and Damnation".

The Harbour

From Castlegate, take the cobbled Shiprow Street down to the north side of the harbour and the Maritime Museum. The building's glass façade provides a superb view of the busy harbour, and its excellent exhibits of the harbour's historical and modern activities place a special accent on the North Sea oil and gas production.

Next door, the old Provost Ross House (1593) displays splendid ship models and nautical paintings. Shiprow continues down to the harbourfront Market Street, where oil-supply ships dock beside old fishing vessels.

The Beach

Aberdeen's beach is just northeast of the city centre. There are two good reasons to go there, especially for children: the great stretch of unpolluted sands and, at 179 Constitution Street behind the Patio Hotel, the Satrosphere, converted from tram sheds into a hands-on science exhibition of technology and modern biology.

Old Aberdeen

This village-like suburb north of the city centre has preserved its medieval cobbled lanes, the 15th-century St Machar's Cathedral—an imposing granite edifice overlooking the River Don—and to the south, university buildings around the fine King's College Chapel (1495).

Deeside

South of Aberdeen, the River Dee meanders west through craggy landscapes of glens and forests to the Grampian and Cairngorm Mountains. The baronial castles along the route have been popular tourist destinations ever since Queen Victoria came in 1848 and bought Balmoral Castle four years later as a royal residence.

Drum Castle

Some 16 km (10 miles) west of Aberdeen, the medieval Drum Castle stands amid 40 ha of magnificent oak and pine forest. This 83 is itself just a remnant of vast woodlands that once fed Aberdeen's shipbuilding industry. Flanked by a handsome Jacobean mansion, the grand battlemented castle-keep dates back to the late 13th century. It was part of the property given by Robert the Bruce to his armour bearer William de Irvine in 1323. It remained in the family's hands for over 650 years, and their portraits and fine Georgian furnishings have been preserved by the National Trust for Scotland.

Crathes Castle

East of the village of Banchory, the castle is built around a classical 16th-century tower house. Highlights of its interior are the painted ceilings in the Chamber of the Muses, the Chamber of the Nine Nobles (Biblical, historical and mythical figures from King David to Julius Caesar and King Arthur) and the haunted Green Lady's Room. Attractive walled gardens have a beautiful array of herbaceous borders and artfully sculpted yew hedges.

Balmoral Castle

The 16th-century tower house, once a stronghold of the Gordon family, was bought in 1852 as a royal residence for Queen Victoria by her husband Prince Albert. It stands amid rolling hills and woodlands near the River Dee, 14 km (9 miles) west of Ballater, where the train station—but not the railway—remains to commemorate the queen's first visit to the region four years earlier. The mansion was rebuilt with all the turrets and flourishes of the Scottish baronial style, using granite quarried from the nearby Glen Gelder. Only the grand ballroom and grounds are open to the public, roughly from early April to late July. There are pony-cart rides in a converted milk float, pony trekking, guided walks organized by the ranger service and salmon-fishing on the Balmoral Estates' stretch of the River Dee.

Braemar and Linn of Dee

This pretty village is best known for its annual Highland Games or "Braemar Gathering", the first dating back to the 11th century, and now held on the first Saturday in September. The village is a popular base for hikers heading 9 km (5 miles) west to the spectacular Linn of Dee, where the river turns into a raging torrent hurling itself through a narrow rocky gorge into the Cairngorms.

Malt Whisky Trail

The trail describes a triangle in the Speyside region around Dufftown at the northern edge of the Cairngorm Mountains. It is the waters of the River Spey and its tributaries that refine such famous

SINGLE MALT

Single malt tastes so good because its production is so meticulous, worth a little study. Malt whisky is made from malted barley. Spirit made from any other grains may be called Scotch Whisky, but barley converted to green malt is what makes single malts special. The kiln with its distinctive pagoda pinnacle is where the green malt is heated over a furnace to dry it out and add the smoky peat flavour.

The next step is the "tea making" in a steel Mash Tun, using hot water to extract useful ingredients for brewing. The brewing or Washback uses yeast to raise the alcohol content to 7%, a substance known as weak beer. This in turn undergoes a first distillation, in the Wash Still, to create a 21% "low wine". Nothing is wasted—this is Scotland we're talking about—so a condenser captures the vapours coming from the stills and turns them into useable liquid.

The second and usually last distillation takes place in the Spirit Still, turning the 28% mixture of "low wine" and unwanted products of earlier distillation (known as "feints") into a spirit at 70% alcohol. This is the stuff that will end up in the casks, but first it has to go through a Spirit Safe. This lovely brass-bound glass case is where the distiller analyses and directs the flow of the product—without ever coming into physical contact with it—before it goes on to the Warehouse.

The Warehouse is the holy of holies. It is generally agreed that three-quarters of a malt whisky's taste comes not from the barley, the water or the peat but from the oak casks in which it is matured. A Scottish single malt's casks are mostly of American white oak, already used to mature bourbon, the rest being of European oak, used to mature sherry. It has something to do with the chemical qualities left in the wood by the cask's previous occupants. No two connoisseurs have the same explanation, but anything coming from the holy of holies is a matter of faith. The appreciation of single malt is practically a religion.

malt whiskies as Glenfiddich and Glenlivet, but also provide great sport for salmon-fishing. The distilleries offer tours and tastings (or for drivers, the alternative of a miniature to taste later).

Dufftown

Any town calling itself the "Malt Whisky Capital of the World" has an understandably bright and breezy atmosphere to it. The splendid clock tower in the middle of the town's Main Square has a tourist office providing all the information you need for visiting your choice among the seven clearly signposted distilleries in the region.

Glenfiddich

On the north side of Dufftown, the Glenfiddich Distillery started up in 1887, but it was only in 1963 that it became the first to market its single malt whisky on a worldwide basis. Unique among local producers, its light, slightly sweet whiskies are bottled on the premises, in the famous tall triangular bottles.

Craigellachie

Just 6 km (4 miles) north of Dufftown at the confluence of the Fiddich and Spey rivers, the village looks out over Thomas Telford's splendid iron bridge (1815). It is home to the Macallan Distillery. You can also visit the Speyside Cooperage, where more than 100,000 oak casks are repaired each year—old being better than new ones for producing the finest quality.

Strathisla Distillery

Beautifully situated on the *strath* (flatland valley) of the River Isla northeast of Dufftown at Keith, the twin pagoda pinnacles of this oldest of the region's distilleries (1786) are the landmark of the celebrated rich-flavoured Chivas Regal. Tours here are self-guided. Teetotallers and drivers can try the coffee and tasty shortbread.

Cardhu

At Knockando, 11 km (7 miles) west of Craigellachie, the picturesque distillery stands right beside the ice-cold spring waters that distinguish Cardhu's special qualities. Pioneered in the 19th century by a woman, the distillery produces a light and smoky whisky matured for a minimum of 12 years.

Glenlivet

In an age of illicit distillers reluctant to pay excise taxes to the English foe, Glenlivet was the first to be licensed, in 1824. The fragrant 12-year malt is produced southwest of Dufftown on the banks of the Livet, a mountain stream that flows into a tributary of the River Spey.

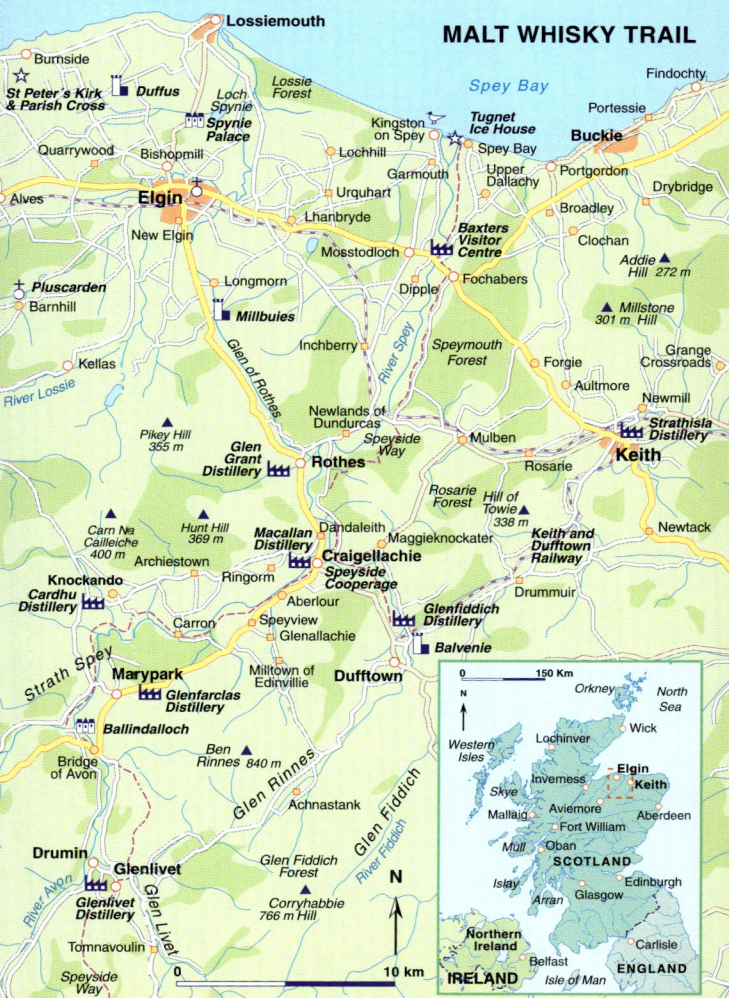

MALT WHISKY TRAIL

Lossiemouth

Burnside
★ St Peter's Kirk & Parish Cross
Duffus
Spynie Palace
Loch Spynie
Lossie Forest
Spey Bay
Findochty
Portessie
Buckie
Kingston on Spey
Tugnet Ice House
Spey Bay

Quarrywood
Bishopmill
Lochhill
Upper Dallachy
Portgordon
Drybridge

Alves
Elgin
New Elgin
Garmouth
Broadley
Clochan

Pluscarden
Barnhill
Longmorn
Lhanbryde
Urquhart
Baxters Visitor Centre
Addie Hill 272 m

Kellas
Millbuies
Inchberry
Mosstodloch
Dipple
Fochabers
Millstone 301 m Hill

Speymouth Forest
Forgie
Aultmore
Grange Crossroads
Newmill

River Spey

Pikey Hill 355 m
Glen Grant Distillery
Rothes
Newlands of Dundurcas
Speyside Way
Mulben
Rosarie
Strathisla Distillery
Keith

Glen of Rothes

Carn Na Cailleiche 400 m
Hunt Hill 369 m
Macallan Distillery
Dandaleith
Rosarie Forest
Hill of Towie 338 m
Newtack

Knockando
Cardhu Distillery
Archiestown
Ringorm
Craigellachie
Speyside Cooperage
Maggieknockater
Keith and Dufftown Railway

Carron
Aberlour
Speyview
Glenallachie
Glenfiddich Distillery
Drummuir

Marypark
Glenfarclas Distillery
Miltown of Edinvillie
Dufftown
Balvenie

Strath Spey

Ballindalloch
Ben Rinnes 840 m
Glen Rinnes

Bridge of Avon
Achnastank

Drumin
Glenlivet
Glenlivet Distillery
Glen Fiddich Forest
Corryhabbie 766 m Hill
Glen Fiddich
River Fiddich

Tomnavoulin
Glen Livet
Speyside Way

River Avon

N

0   10 km

Spey Bay

SCOTLAND inset

0   150 Km
N
Orkney
North Sea
Western Isles
Lochinver
Wick
Skye
Inverness
Elgin
Keith
Mallaig
Aviemore
Aberdeen
Mull
Fort William
Oban
SCOTLAND
Islay
Edinburgh
Arran
Glasgow
Northern Ireland
Carlisle
IRELAND
Belfast
Isle of Man
ENGLAND

THE HIGHLANDS

Glencoe, Fort William, Road to the Isles, Inverness and surroundings, Loch Ness, Glen Shiel, Wester Ross, North Coast

For many people, the Highlands are what Scotland is all about. For them, places like Edinburgh and Glasgow, even the most popular islands. are just the icing on the cake. The purple and green mountains and misty glens, the peat moors and craggy cliffs, silver-blue lochs and sparkling trout and salmon streams—they are all here. This is the real stuff. Bound on three sides by water—the North Sea and Atlantic Ocean—the Highlands do after all account for two-thirds of Scotland's land area. The only towns of any size are Inverness and Fort William, and fewer visitors make it all the way up here, compared with more southerly destinations. But that, for *aficionados*, is a major part of the attraction. Apart from a few mob scenes around places like Loch Ness, the Highlands' remoteness and tranquillity stay blessedly unspoiled.

Beyond the Grampians, the southern part of the Highlands proper starts out from the lovely and historically tragic Glencoe and then follows the long lochs of the Great Glen 100 km (60 miles) from Loch Linnhe in the west at Fort William, northeast via Loch Ness to Inverness. The western region takes in the picturesque Road to the Isles (of Skye and the Western Isles) and the more northerly mountains and sea loch inlets of Wester Ross. The far north coast across to the mainland's northernmost tip at John o'Groats is wild and windy, while the east coast has gentler green pastures, woodlands and a few long sandy beaches around the Firths of Dornoch, Moray and Cromarty.

Glencoe

This magnificent valley in the Grampian Mountains makes a perfect introduction to the Highlands for people driving the A82 highway north from Glasgow. The glen's idyllic beauty—green and rock-strewn mountains disappearing in misty cloud above tranquil lochs—makes all the more poignant the tragic events that unrolled here 300 years ago. The road turns west from the bracken-covered bogs of Rannoch Moor to cross Glen Etive and follow the River Coe past the landmark pyramidal mountain of

The castle of Eilean Donan makes a perfect movie setting.

89

Buachaille Etive Mór (say *boo-achil ay-tyu more*): "great herdsman of Etive", 1,022 m (3,353 ft) high.

At the west end of the valley, on the main road near the village of Glencoe, visit the brand new Glencoe Visitor Centre to pick up information and trail maps. Scaling big Buachaille and other mountains here is strictly for experienced climbers, but there are many simpler well-marked walks which reveal the glen's beauty and historical interest. Red deer, pine marten, stoats and weasels may be seen here, while birdwatchers look out for buzzard, sparrowhawk, kestrel and an occasional golden eagle.

An Torr and Signal Rock

These rocky outcrops are just a half-hour's walk through the woods and back. An Torr provides lovely views up the glen and over to ruins of the clan chief's summer house. Signal Rock was possibly used in ancient times as a place to warn of danger, as it could be seen from all sides of the glen.

GLENCOE MASSACRE

The organized massacre at Glencoe on February 13, 1692 of 38 members of the MacDonald clan has been depicted in English historical accounts as yet another brutal incident in the centuries-long bloody feud between the MacDonalds and the Campbells. To the Scots of Glencoe, it was not that simple. There were indeed a dozen Campbells among the 130 government troops that carried out the treacherous killings. And the MacDonalds of the time, no angels themselves, were notoriously violent brigands and cattle-rustlers, their victims often members of the Campbell clan. However, these were soldiers under orders from King William III's Lord Advocate, John Dalrymple. They had been sent to "make an example" of a hostile Jacobite clan which had failed to meet a deadline to pay allegiance to the English throne. The Campbells' traditional hatred of the Mac-Donalds became a military means to a political end. Following traditional Highland hospitality, the troops were billeted in the homes of MacDonalds whose Glencoe leader was related to the troops' commanding officer. After waiting ten days, the troops received the order to slaughter their hosts—men, women and even babies. Said Dalrymple: "A nit, if allowed to survive, will grow into a louse." Of the 300 who escaped to the hills, many more died of exposure to the bitter winter.

Devil's Staircase

This famous zigzagging path is part of the long-disused military road to Kinlochleven that was the curse of the government troops who had to build it. Starting out 10 km (6 miles) east of the Visitor Centre from beside Altnafeadh Cottage, follow the well-worn trail to the summit ridge for splendid views of the Buachaille mountain. The path is followed by the ramblers' West Highland Way from Glasgow to Fort William.

Fort William

Superbly situated on Loch Linnhe in the shadow of the formidable Ben Nevis, the town founded in honour of William III in 1655 is a popular gateway to the Highlands.

The West Highland Museum on Cameron Square offers a lively introduction to the region's history and way of life. Scottish literature buffs may be intrigued by the Spanish rifle used in the murder of a local tax-collector, inspiring the plot of Robert Louis Stevenson's adventure novel, *Kidnapped*.

On the same square, the tourist office provides details of boat cruises on Loch Linnhe from the town pier, as well as scenic day trips on the Jacobite Steam Train along Loch Eil via Glenfinnan to and from the west coast at Mallaig. The train played the role of the Hogwarts Express in the Harry Potter films.

Ben Nevis

Britain's highet mountain at 1,344 m (4,409 ft) is also its most popular and most treacherous. Snow is likely to fall at the top any time of year, so even the hundreds who hike to the summit in summer should take the proper precautions regarding footwear, warm clothing and sticking to the marked paths. Experienced mountaineers have several options, but the common mortal starts out southeast of Fort William in Glen Nevis from Achintree Farm. The Scottish Mountaineering Club reckons this "easy" route takes 3 hours and 50 minutes, but beginners should figure on 5 hours—and 3 hours back down. On the proverbial clear day at the top, the views really are stupendous, especially south to the peaks of Glencoe.

Road to the Isles

The Road to the Isles—an 80-km (48-mile) stretch of the A830 highway from Fort William to the west-coast ferry port of Mallaig —passes through some of the Highlands' most beautiful countryside. It runs along the mountainous north shore of Loch Eil out to the Arisaig peninsula before turning north to Mallaig. 91

The grand West Highland Railway follows the same route.

Glenfinnan

In an enchanting location 30 km (18 miles) west of Fort William, at the head of Loch Shiel, Glenfinnan is where Bonnie Prince Charlie raised his red and white silk standard one fine August day to launch the Jacobite uprising in 1745. The campaign ended in bloody defeat eight months later at Culloden. On a monument overlooking the loch, the statue of a clansman in battledress pays tribute to the men who died following the prince into battle. The whole valiant and sad story is told at the Visitor Centre.

If you arrive by train from Fort William you'll get a first-hand look at the town's most imposing structure, the Glenfinnan Viaduct (1901), 380 m (1247 ft) long, curving around the head of the River Finnan valley. The tallest of its 21 arches is 30 m (98 ft) high. The station itself doubles as a railway museum.

Arisaig

Two attractions here: cruises from the harbour out to the Inner Hebrides isles of Muck, Eigg and Rhum; and great expanses of fine white sandy beaches around the bay. It was here that Robert Louis Stevenson met one-eyed, peg-legged Long John Silver working as a builder on a lighthouse designed by Stevenson's father and turned him into a pirate in *Treasure Island*.

Mallaig

The town at the end of the Road to the Isles is a busy fishing port as well as ferry-port for the Isle of Skye and Western Isles. The town's chief attraction is the Mallaig Marine World near the harbour on local sea life. Swimmers may want to seek out the sandy cove just north of the town at Mallaigmore.

HIGHLIGHTS

- **Glencoe**: Highlands' historic and most beautiful glen
- **Ben Nevis**: Britain's highest mountain
- **Loch Ness**: even without the monster, the loch is lovely
- **Applecross Peninsula**: adventurous drive with spectacular rewards
- **Inverewe Gardens**: exotic luxuriance on a craggy coast
- **Corrieshalloch Gorge**: tree-covered gorge with spectacular waterfall

Buachaille Etive Mór, "the great herdsman of Etive" guards the memories of Glencoe.

Inverness and surroundings

The capital of the Highlands is also its principal gateway, lying at the northern tip of the Great Glen where the River Ness flows into the Moray Firth: *Inver* means river mouth. Surprisingly, it was not granted city status until December 2000. Boosted by a modern shopping centre, this is one of the few northern Scottish towns with a growing population—currently over 66,500.

City Centre

The 19th-century neo-Gothic Town House stands on the High Street. Its old Mercat Cross shows that for centuries this was the main hub of what is now a pedestrian-zoned shopping centre. Towering above all is the red sandstone Inverness Castle, also built largely in the 19th century on the site of fortresses successively destroyed by Robert the Bruce at the turn of the 14th century and the Jacobites in 1746, among others. It is now a courthouse but stages a popular pageant in 18th-century costume on the esplanade. On the terrace is a statue of Flora MacDonald, looking wistfully south.

Below the castle on Castle Wynd (next to the tourist office), Inverness Museum is devoted to 93 the region's geography, history and folklore.

North of the Town House on Church Street is the town's oldest building, the step-gabled Abertarff House (1593), restored by the National Trust for Scotland and now housing a gallery for contemporary Scottish artists.

Caledonian Canal and River Ness

Designed by Thomas Telford in the early 19th century to link the Highlands' east and west coasts, it serves mainly now for leisurely cruises south to Loch Ness. Walkers can enjoy a stroll along the tree-lined towpaths past the picturesque locks. Close by, River Ness—popular for its salmon fishing—offers rambles to the parkland of the Ness Islands, linked by footbridges.

Strathpeffer

This genteel Victoria spa resort 20 km (12 miles) north of Inverness via the A9 and A834 attracts visitors as much for the walks it offers in the pretty wooded foothills of BenWyvis as for the restorative powers of its natural sulphurous springs. The picturesque Pump Room, Sampling Pavilion and majestic turreted hotels recall the days when the resort attracted ailing or hypochondriac gentry

---

DRIVING SINGLE-TRACK ROADS

The further north they go, drivers in Scotland must watch out for two things: the distracting hazard of increasingly beautiful unspoiled countryside, and the challenge this presents to handling the narrow, winding single-track roads. The latter need pose no problem to attentive drivers observing the traditional etiquette:

• On both sides of the road, passing places are provided at regular distances, sign-posted with a "Passing Place" panel or occasionally a black and white striped pole.

• These are *not* parking places, so do not use them for a photo opportunity or other reasons for a pit-stop.

• Remember: the law on driving on the left still applies. If the passing place ahead of you is on the right and you will reach it before an oncoming car, stop on the left side of the road opposite the passing place—it can be highly dangerous to pull across to the right.

• To allow traffic to flow freely, drivers should be neither hesitant nor inconsiderate, particularly when going downhill with traffic approaching.

There is nothing we can do about that wonderful scenery.

from all over Europe. They came by train to the Old Railway Station, now converted to craft workshops and the Highland Museum of Childhood displaying both cheery folklore and the darker memories of child labour.

Culloden

A short drive east of Inverness is the battlefield of Culloden Moor where, on April 16, 1746, some 1,500 Highlanders died at the hands of the English. On the battle site, the armies' positions are marked by flags, simple headstones mark the clansmen's graves, and the Field of the English marks the spot where about 50 English soldiers are buried. Next to the restored 18th-century Leanach cottage, a visitor centre tells the battle's bloody stories. Guided tours are organized from Inverness—from the tourist office and by Guide Friday buses from Bridge Street.

Cawdor Castle

Despite the hype, the castle 13 km (8 miles) east of Culloden is *not* where Shakespeare's Macbeth, Thane of Cawdor, carried out his dastardly deeds. But who cares? Its crow-stepped gables, battlemented castle-keep, dungeons, pepperpot turrets and secret passages seem *right* and are a lot of fun. Stylishly restored in the 19th century, the original castle was built in the 14th century, 300 years after Macbeth died, and the Cawdor family still live there (outside the summer months). Best of all are the spacious grounds, with walled garden, the topiary maze and the nature trails through the woods. One thing Shakespeare did get right was when he wrote:

> *This Castle hath a pleasant*
> *seat; the air*
> *Nimbly and sweetly*
> *recommends itself*
> *Unto our gentle senses…*

Aviemore

Sports enthusiasts—in summer and winter—head for Aviemore, 50 km (30 miles) southeast of Inverness, but an easy drive along the A9 motorway. Surrounded by spectacular mountain scenery, Britain's premier ski resort makes up in modern amenities for what the village itself may lack in romantic charm. High above Loch Morlich in the Glenmore Forest Park, with its herd of reindeer, the main ski area is reached by the CairnGorm Mountain Railway which opened in 2001. In summer, the forest's first-class cross-country skiing trails offer splendid rambles, biking, riding and pony trekking. Loch Morlich has grand facilities for canoeing, windsurfing and sailing. Anglers go for the salmon and trout in the River Spey.

95

Loch Ness

It is in any case a very pretty loch. Even if there is no monster in this longest of the four lochs making up the Great Glen following the geological fault-line from Fort William to Inverness, Loch Ness is worth a visit. Measuring 36 km (nearly 22 miles) in length and going down to a depth of 240 m (787 ft), the loch also boasts Britain's largest volume of fresh water. Most bus tours go down the tree-lined western highway A82 to the loch's southwestern tip at Fort Augustus, via the gaudy souvenir shops and dubious exhibition centres of Drumnadrochit—the "monster observation point" at the 14th-century ruin of Urquhart Castle—and the pretty village of Invermoriston. Loch cruises are available at Drumnadrochit.

For monster-phobes, the single-track B862 road along the eastern shore offers better views of the loch and is, of course, much less busy. At Dores, turn inland southeast up to the beautiful little Loch Mhor and the woodlands lining the route back down to Fort Augustus. The fort was replaced in the 19th century by a now empty Benedictine Abbey, but the village can claim the loch's best-looking statue of the monster.

MONSTER?

Reports of Nessie, as she is popularly known, go back to the 6th century when the great monastic missionary St Columba is said to have pacified the beast after it attacked one of his monks. Over the centuries, local residents talked about the weird things they saw gliding through the waters, most clearly when there was a full moon. Sightings increased exponentially in the 1930s when the A82 highway was built. People never said they saw more than one, so Nessie—or *Nessiteras rhombopteryx* in "scientific" terms—either never goes out with her partner or is a solitary survivor of the otherwise long-extinct plesiosaur, by now at least 1,400 years old. Photographs and film of sightings on display at Drumnadrochit have been demonstrated to be fakes.

Glen Shiel

From Loch Ness via Fort Augustus or Inveriston, the westbound highway links up with the A87, a popular and picturesque route passing through the beautiful Glen Shiel to the Skye Road Bridge, perhaps the sole, but very good *raison d'être* for the village of Kyle of Lochalsh. On the way are several exhilarating hiking trails along the mountain ridges.

Looks as though Nessie doesn't much like having her photo taken.

The two best known are the Five Sisters Traverse on the north side of Glen Shiel and the Kintail Ridge to the south, starting out from the Cluanie Inn at the western end of Loch Cluanie. A little effort is needed to get up to the ridges, but thereafter the going is easy and the views over the mountains and lochs absolutely stunning. Before setting out, hikers are advised to pick up information and detailed trail maps at the tourist office in Inverness or Fort William.

Eilean Donan Castle

With its mountain backdrop west of Glen Shiel on the north shore of Loch Duich, this is truly Hollywood's idea of a romantic castle. A narrow stone bridge takes visitors out to the battlemented fort at the water's edge. It began life in the 13th century as a defence against attack from the Vikings, was blown up by the English in 1719, then rebuilt in the 20th century and made available for films including *Highlander* and a James Bond film.

Plockton

Much appreciated by painters for the palm trees and gaily painted houses hugging the harbour, this charming little village was home to crofters until they

97

were shipped out by the Clearances at the end of the 18th century. It enjoyed brief prosperity as a fishing port and now bathes in the afterglow of its brief fame as the setting for a popular BBC TV series, *Hamish Macbeth*.

Wester Ross

The handsome unspoiled west coastal region—"Ross", from the Gaelic *Rois*, means headland—is made up of mountainous peninsulas separated by fjord-like sea lochs. It stretches north from Lochcarron (a good place to stock up on hiking trail maps and other regional information at the tourist office) to Ullapool, ferry port for the Western Isles and the remote fishing village of Achiltibuie.

Applecross Peninsula

From Lochcarron, the 30 km (18 mile) drive over the Applecross Peninsula is an exhilarating experience, to say the least. As the A896 single-track road turns north, the route strikes out due west across Bealach na Bà (Cattle Pass) on a spine-tingling old drove road of hairpin bends. It climbs to 626 m (2,053 ft) and can claim to be Scotland's highest paved road, passing between formidable buttresses of sheer rock. All along the way, the effort is rewarded by magnificent views of the Applecross Hills and over the sea to Skye and the peaks of

Cuillin. Parking areas make it possible for drivers to calm their nerves and share the joy with their passengers. Flowers here include spotted orchid, wild iris and alpine ladies' mantle.

The seaside village of Applecross, where the Irish monk Maelrubha (or Molroy) built a monastery in 673 on his mission to the Picts, is a peaceful community of whitewashed cottages clustered around its hospitable inn and B&Bs. Out in the bay, you may spot seals and an occasional dolphin.

Loch Torridon

From the charming fishing port of Shieldaig, the A896 road runs along the south shore of the sea loch towards the mountains of Liathach, culminating at 1,054 m (3,458 ft) and Beinn Alligin, 984 m (3,228 ft). With their red sandstone slopes rising to peaks of white quartzite, they form a dramatic backdrop to the village of Torridon. The National Trust for Scotland's Countryside Centre there provides excellent information on the area's flowers and wildlife and trail maps for the mountains. Beginners are advised to join the guided walks of the NTS Ranger Service.

Loch Maree

North of Torridon, pine-covered island and hillside nature reserves make this one of the Highlands' most beautiful sea lochs, best explored from the village of Kinlochewe.

On the loch's south shore, Beinn Eighe was Britain's first National Nature Reserve. The Visitor Centre has information about the pine marten, red deer, wild cat and mountain hare in the reserve's ancient pinewoods, as well as the alpine flora on the higher slopes. Birdwatchers look out for golden eagles, kestrels, peregrine falcons and sparrowhawks. Around the islands are porpoises, dolphins, seals and otters.

Gairloch

Sandy beaches, boat cruises and a good golf course make this one of the most popular summer resorts in Wester Ross. The Gairloch Heritage Museum offers a good introduction to the region's archaeology, geology and folklore.

Inverewe Garden

Blessed by the warm currents and breezes of the Gulf Stream flowing past Loch Ewe, the 20 ha of Inverewe Garden bring together flora from the world over. A 5-km (3-mile) labyrinth of paths leads you in and out of a sprawling walled garden, pond garden, peat banks, majestic Rhododendron Walk and Azalea Walk blooming in May and June, astonishing herbaceous gardens at their exuberant best in high summer, New Zealand scree, Chinese, Japanese, Himalayan and North and South American gardens. They were created in the 19th century by Osgood Mackenzie, whose mother and brother bought the rocky and barren promontory for him when he was 20, upon the death of his father. To make the garden possible, he planted shelterbelts of pine, reclaimed land from the sea and imported soil from Ireland. The luxuriance makes a stark contrast to the craggy coast flanking the estate that is now administered by the National Trust for Scotland.

Gruinard Bay

North across the peninsula from Inverewe, the little village of Laide makes a delightful base from which to explore the lovely sandy coves north to Mellon Udrigle and Opinan and south around the bay

Corrieshalloch Gorge

Just south of Braemore on the A835, this splendid gorge is 1.5 km (almost a mile) long and 61 m (200 ft) deep, with a wonderful array of trees and flowery shrubs growing from the sheer rock face on either side of the chasm. The River Broom, plunging 46 m (150 ft) over the Falls of Measach, can normally be 99

Ullapool was custom-designed on a neat grid-plan by Thomas Telford to exploit a boom in the herring fishing industry.

viewed from a swaying suspension bridge built downstream in the 19th century or from a more recent and less adventurous viewing platform, but the site is temporarily closed for safety reasons.

Ullapool

The ferry terminal for Stornoway and the Western Isles is also a bustling fishing port established on Loch Broom in 1788. The tourist office provides good information about hikes into the surrounding glens and mountains and wildlife cruises around Loch Broom, Annat Bay and to the uninhabited Summer Isles to spot seabirds, porpoises and dolphins.

North Coast

North of Ullapool, the road to the British mainland's northernmost parts leads through some of the country's most dramatic landscapes—jagged peaks rising abruptly from windswept moorland, enchanting villages nestling in isolated valleys, and fishing hamlets overlooking secluded sandy coves.

Turn west at the lovely Loch Assynt, running 10 km (6 miles) between the peaks of Beinn Gharb to the south and Quinag to the north. Beyond it is the busy port of Lochinver, popular with anglers both for shore and deepsea fishing.

Either the coast road (single track past spectacular cliffs and offshore rock pillars) or the faster A837 brings you to Kylesku and its handsome modern road bridge spanning the mouths of the Glencoul and Glendhu lochs.

Further north, Kinlochbervie fishing port lies west of the main road, a good base for exploring the crofters' villages of Oldshoremore and Blairmore and their sandy beaches, most beautiful of all being Sandwood Bay.

From Kinlochbervie, the coast road passes through Durness, a crofters' village from which hardy hikers make it out to the wild and windy Cape Wrath, the mainland's northwestern counterpart to John o'Groats.

To the east, Tongue is a pretty town founded by Norsemen, overlooked by the ruins of their Varick castle. At low tide, take a walk on the sandflats on the Kyle (narrow strait) of Tongue.

Thurso (from the Norse for Thor's River) is the closest thing to a real town on the north coast. Visit Old St Peter's Church and Thurso Heritage Museum near the harbour. Nearby Scrabster port has a ferry service to the Orkney Islands.

On the road to John o'Groats, the Castle of Mey was the Caithness residence of the late Queen Mother, and is the northernmost castle on the British mainland.

John o'Groats

This nondescript town at the northeastern tip of the British mainland is 1,398 km (839 miles) from Land's End, the southwestern tip of Cornwall. You can visit The Last House and its small museum. West of John o'Groats, the lighthouse and military buildings of Dunnet Head are further north (though not so far from Land's End), but Duncansby Head to the east offers grandiose cliffs and rock formations for a more satisfyingly dramatic climax for an end-to-end trek.

MORE THAN ONE GROAT

John o'Groats is named after Dutchman Jan de Groot. In 1496, James IV granted him the ferry franchise from the harbour here to the island of Orkney. The octagonal hotel recalls the eight-sided house which de Groot is said to have built to enable his eight quarrelling sons each to come in by his own door. It is more fancifully claimed that the ferryman gave his name to the silver groat, the coin which the Scottish government fixed as the fare for the trip to Orkney. That may have been the price, but the groat appeared in Britain at least a century earlier.

101

Stretching northeast of the British mainland, the two archipelagos of Orkney and Shetland are very much self-contained worlds apart on the Scottish scene. In custom and character, the fiercely independent-minded peoples have more in common with their Norse origins than the Highlands. Historically, the Scottish influence has always come more from southern Lowlanders than the Gaelic neighbours. The dialects maintain Scandinavian roots—while people may discern in the English *lingua franca* a distinctive "Welsh" lilt.

The topography of Orkney, except for Hoy's dramatic crags and soaring cliffs, provides for fertile farmland across low rolling hills, with few trees due to the strong prevailing winds. The streams are good for trout fishing. Further north, Shetland has a more rugged, even mountainous terrain with deep fjord-like inlets. The economy is principally devoted to fishing, supplemented by the North Sea oil boom and its offshoots in the computer industry.

The red sandstone cliffs on the west coast of Hoy—an Old Norse name for "high island".

Both Orkney and Shetland have impressive remains of Stone Age settlements dating back to 4000 BC. Orkney has just two towns of any size, the capital Kirkwall and the ferry port Stromness, while the Shetlanders have only their capital, Lerwick, serving as ferry port and shopping centre.

Orkney Islands
Of the more than 70 islands and islets just 32 km (19 miles) north of the Scottish mainland, only 20 are inhabited. Most of the 19,600 Orcadians, as they are known (after the archipelago's ancient classical name of Orcades), are concentrated on the island they call Mainland. The capital, Kirkwall, lies on the isthmus between the East Mainland and the larger West Mainland, on which the principal sights are situated, all within fairly easy reach of the ferry port of Stromness.

Stromness
With its sandstone piers, private wharves and 18th-century slate-roof gabled houses, the old harbour on the sheltered Hamnavoe inlet is itself the town's major attraction. In 1670 the Hudson's Bay Company chose Stromness as its first and last port of call for

103

GETTING AROUND

Car ferries from Aberdeen, Gills Bay (near John o'Groats) or Scrabster (near Thurso on the north Highlands coast) tend to be expensive, so we recommend renting a car on the islands or using the pretty good bus service.

the transatlantic passage to Canada. The imposing Warehouse near the new ferry terminal bears witness to the prosperity this brought the town when troubles with Napoleon made it safer for merchant ships to avoid the English Channel.

The main street takes on half a dozen names as it extends north along the waterfront. At the southern end stands the cannon that was fired to signal the arrival of a company ship.

On Albert Street, Stromness Museum is devoted to the islands' natural history as well as a colourful collection of relics from shipwrecks, most notably from the German High Seas Fleet scuttled in Scapa Flow in 1919. On the pier at the north end of Victoria Street, the Pier Arts Centre exhibits both the works of local artists and an impressive permanent collection of British art by Barbara Hepworth, Ben Nicholson and Patrick Heron.

East of the waterfront, narrow lanes climb up the Brinkies Brae hill, one of them, flanked by high walls, known as the Khyber Pass.

Stenness and Brodgar

Northeast of Stromness on the A965 highway to Kirkwall, the Stones of Stenness originally formed a circle of 12 standing monoliths, of which just four still very impressive stones have survived. Dating back to 3000 BC, the tallest is almost 6 m (19 ft) high, surrounded by a henge or bank of earth with a ditch and approached by two causeways. East of the circle, whose purpose remains undetermined, a path leads to the Barnhouse Settle-

---

HIGHLIGHTS

- **Stromness**: colourful harbour dating back to 1670
- **Stenness and Brodgar**: prehistoric Standing Stones
- **Maeshowe**: ancient burial chamber in the Maidens' Mound
- **Italian Chapel**: astonishing wartime work of art and faith
- **Lerwick**: Shetland's pleasant, easy-going capital
- **Jarlshof**: dwellings from Stone Age to Vikings

ment, remains of a Stone Age hamlet. Archaeologists have concluded that the buildings were destroyed not long after they were built, and have surmised that they may have housed itinerant workmen who left the area after completing the Stones of Stenness.

Northwest of the circle is a lone monolith, the towering Watch Stone, 6.5 m (21 ft) high, and beyond that the Ring o' Brodgar (2500 BC) beautifully located on a natural embankment dividing the saltwater Loch Stenness to the west from the freshwater Loch Harray to the east. Of the original 60 stones, which formed a perfect circle 110 m (360 ft) in diameter, 27 stones are still standing, again surrounded by a ditch with two causeways.

Maeshowe

Beneath its grassy mound a short walk northeast of the Stones of Stenness, the ancient chambered tomb of Maeshowe (pronounced *mayz-ow*) was built around 2700 BC, making it at least as old as Egypt's first pyramid (usually dated 2680 BC). Beautifully preserved in its interior, the monumental burial mound is regarded by archaeologists as one of the most important such structures in Europe. Get your entrance tickets across the road at Tormiston Mill.

The entrance passageway at the southwest side of the mound,

MAIDEN'S MOUND

In old Orcadian dialect, *maeshowe* meant maiden's mound. Island historian Ernest Marwick says of the maidens that "at one time every young girl within a mile of Maeshowe had to take a *kaesy* (basket) of ashes to the top of the mound each full moon, empty it there and urinate on the ashes." Ashes and urine were used on Orkney to foretell the future, as modern fortune-tellers read the patterns left by tea-leaves in a cup.

the central tomb and its three side chambers are all formed from massive sandstone slabs. The tomb is aligned so that on the day of the winter solstice the last rays of the sun shine directly over the top of a nearby solitary monolith known as the Barnhouse Stone and through the Maeshowe passageway to light up the inner burial chamber. In the annual cycle at this far northern latitude, the "death" of the midwinter sun signalled the return of life.

Rediscovered in 1861, Maeshowe had been emptied by tombraiders over the centuries, leaving only part of a human skull and a few horse bones. In the 12th century, Vikings left graffiti in their twig-rune alphabet, 30 of which still remain. Like graffiti every-

105

where, some just record the names of their writers: "Haermund Hardaxe", "Tholfir Kolbeinsson"; others are romantic tributes—to "Ingebjork the fair widow"—and others are too obscene to be recorded here.

Skara Brae

The fascinating remains of the 5,000-year-old fishing and farming village of Skara Brae stand above the white sands of Skaill Bay. The stone houses were built into the shelter of what had been the village's mounds of midden (now grassed over). The roofs have gone, but around the hearth, stone box-beds, dressers, kitchen pantries and other furnishings are still there in dwellings linked by stone-walled passageways. Only the village workshop stands apart, separated from the houses by an open courtyard.

As an introductory guide to how the villagers of Skara Brae lived, the Visitor Centre presents a full-size recreation of a typical house, complete with a fire burning in the hearth. When it was built, around 3100 BC, Skara Brae stood inland, not as now on the brink of the bay.

The Skara Brae entry ticket includes access to the sprawling buildings of Skaill House, just inland. Dating back in part to the 17th century, they were once the residence of the laird of Skaill.

Yesnaby

A bracing clifftop walk south of the Bay of Skaill leads to the spectacular sandstone cliffs of Yesnaby with their impressive rocky outcrops, the most formidable being a sea stack known as Yesnaby Castle, a perennial challenge to audacious climbers. The beautiful wildflowers here in spring and summer include the little purple Scottish primrose, pink thrift and spotted orchid. Beware of the fiercely protective seabirds in nesting season.

Brough of Birsay

Out on its tidal island at the northwestern corner of West Mainland, remains of this ancient Pictish and medieval Viking settlement are accessible for a couple of hours either side of high tide (daily times available from Stromness and Kirkwall tourist offices). The Picts lived here in the 7th and 8th centuries, most of their buildings lying beneath the Vikings' sandstone houses built from the 9th to the 13th centuries. (Erosion by the waves has buried much of the original village.) Centre of attention is the 12th-century St Peter's Church, in which recesses for the altars and apse and stone seats along the walls can still be seen. The Visitor Centre will also direct you to what was once probably a sauna and bathhouse.

The first stage in traditional whisky making, still carried out in Orkney, is to spread the barley on a malting floor to allow the grains to germinate.

A walk up to the lighthouse, now unmanned, is rewarded with a great view over the Atlantic coastline.

Kirkwall
On the neck of land where West and East Mainland meet, the capital of Orkney looks distinctly Scandinavian. Its modern harbour, ferry port for the northern isles, is less picturesque than that of Stromness, but it boasts two splendid medieval edifices, St Magnus Cathedral and the Earl's Palace. Begun in 1137, the handsome red sandstone Cathedral is considered one of Scotland's finest Romanesque churches.

Guided tours take you up a narrow spiral staircase to explore the church's upper reaches, most notably the monumental west window. Memorials in the southeast corner of the church pay homage to the best-known writers of Orkney—George Mackay Brown, Edwin Muir and Eric Linklater. The Earl's Palace was built in 1607 by Earl Patrick Stewart, brutally employing slave labour to erect what is nonetheless, even in its present ruined state, an outstanding Renaissance castle.

Opposite the cathedral, the 16th-century Tankerness House is the home of Orkney Museum, 107 tracing the islands' history and folklore.

Kirkwall's bustling shopping centre is along Bridge and Albert Streets.

East Mainland

Mainland's smaller eastern peninsula is given over mostly to farming, with a few fishing villages and fine clifftop walks for birdwatchers along the northeastern coast around Mull Head—plentiful guillemots, razorbills, kittiwakes and puffins from May to late August. Since World War II, the islands south of East Mainland have been linked by a series of four causeways known as the Churchill Barriers. These were built as anti-submarine barriers to protect the British fleet based in the bay of Scapa Flow, after a German U-boat torpedoed *HMS Royal Oak* in October, 1939.

Italian Chapel

This astonishing work of art and faith stands on tiny Lambholm, first of the islands to be linked to East Mainland by the Churchill Barrier causeways. It was built by Italian prisoners of war brought to Orkney after their capture in North Africa in 1942. Working on the causeways, their Camp 60 used some of the surplus concrete and other materials to create the chapel out of two Nissen huts. Domenico Chiocchetti, from the

SCAPA FLOW

Orkney's great natural harbour is formed by the coasts of West and East Mainland with further shelter from the southern islands. Controlling the passage between north Britain and Norway, it was the British Navy's chief base throughout two world wars. Many of its 1940s defences are still visible—half-submerged blockships, the Churchill Barrier causeways and coastal gun-battery placements. At the end of World War I, Germany was forced to surrender almost its entire High Seas Fleet, sailing 74 ships into the confines of Scapa Flow. Profiting from the British guard squadron's departure on torpedo practice on Midsummer's Day, 1919, Admiral Ludwig von Reuter ordered all the ships to be scuttled rather than let them fall into the hands of the victorious Allies. Scarpering back when the alarm was sounded, the British could only save by beaching 23 of the vessels. While many were subsequently raised in salvage operations, enough ships remain on the sea bed to this day to make Scapa Flow one of the world's great sites for diving (excursions organized out of Stromness).

north Italian village of Moena, designed the splendid *trompe l'œil* façade, complete with belfry, the interior's vivid murals, monumental altar and painted glass windows, while the sanctuary's grand wrought-iron roodscreen is the work of the camp's blacksmith Palumbo. Chiocchetti's equestrian statue of St George and the Dragon is fashioned from barbed wire coated with concrete.

Shetland Islands

The landscape is composed of craggy, rocky cliffs along a deep indented coastline of inlets with a wild and beautiful interior of sheep pastures among steep green hills. The inlets, known locally as *voes*, reach so far inland that nowhere in Shetland is more than 5 km (3 miles) from the sea, which is visible practically everywhere. As on Orkney, blustery winds leave few trees, yet temperatures are surprisingly mild, mellowed by the North Atlantic Current that is an extension of the Gulf Stream. Only 15 of the 100 or so Shetland islands are inhabited, with a total population of 22,000. Most of them live on the elongated Mainland island, location of the only town, Lerwick, and Shetland's most important archaeological sites.

At Mainland's northern end is the Sullom Voe oil terminal, where Shetlanders tap into the wealth of North Sea oil and cross their fingers that it will last. On the southern tip is Shetland's airport, at Sumburgh.

Further south, on the way to Orkney, is Fair Isle, famous for its decorative knitwear (on sale in Lerwick) and now also protected by the National Trust for Scotland as a bird-sanctuary for the 335 species spotted there.

Lerwick

The capital's charming main road is Commercial Street, known to townspeople just as "da Street"— as Lerwick itself is known to Shetlanders just as "da Toon". It

SHETLAND PONIES

Still bred all over Shetland, but mostly up on the remote isle of Unst, they come in all colours but only one size: tiny. The islands' harsh climate and scarce grazing have combined to produce the world's hardiest little ponies. At an average height of 102 cm (40 in), the Shetland is indeed the smallest natural-bred horse in the world. In the 1850s, industrialists exploited them for their size by sending them through the tunnels of English coal mines. Now they have a quieter, pleasanter life as children's ponies, much prized for their gentle temperament.

THIS IS AS FAR AS IT GOES

Shetland boasts the northernmost point of the British Isles. Just beyond the tip of the wild and windy isle of Unst—where they breed the best Shetland ponies—is Muckle Flugga lighthouse (built by Robert Louis Stevenson's father Thomas) and beyond that is the rocky outcrop of Out Stack. And beyond that is the North Pole.

winds its way parallel to the harbour front and Esplanade, with most of the old buildings and merchants' *lodberry* mansions-cum-warehouses at the southern end. On piers extending from these lodberries, the merchants dealt with Dutch herring boats, a trade that was the source of the town's foundation in the 17th century. Further south is the pretty Bain's Beach.

From the heart of "da Street", narrow lanes, known as *closses*, climb uphill to the 19th-century "new town", dominated by Lerwick's most imposing building, the Town Hall on Hillhead. Just opposite, housed above the town library, Shetland Museum traces a very nautical history of the islands.

To the north, the largely 18th-century Fort Charlotte, named after the wife of George III, offers a fine view from its battlements over the harbour.

Scalloway

Over on the Atlantic coast, the quiet little fishing village 10 km (6 miles) west of Lerwick is Shetland's first capital. Overlooking the harbour is the corbelled ruin of Scalloway Castle, built in 1600 by Earl Patrick Stewart's slave labour (like his palace in Kirkwall. The little Scalloway Museum on Main Street tells the moving World War II story of the "Shetland Bus"—the name given to Norwegian fishing boats bringing guns and ammunition to Norway's resistance fighters and returning with their refugees to the safety of Scalloway.

Mousa Broch

On the isle of Mousa just off the east coast of South Mainland, 24 km (14 miles) south of Lerwick, this 2,000-year-old fortified tower is one of the tallest and best preserved in Scotland. Standing in a green meadow overlooking the sea, the 13-m (43-ft) *broch* is formed from two concentric walls of locally quarried stone. A low passage leads to the inner chamber where a stone water tank has been hollowed from the bedrock. Between the inner and outer walls, a narrow spiral staircase (take a torch) takes you past

Shetland ponies have lived on these islands for 2000 years, their thick coats protecting them from the elements.

six storage-galleries to the roof-top parapet.

Jarlshof

At Sumburgh Head on Mainland's southern tip, this prehistoric settlement takes its name from the 17th-century Old House of Sumburgh which Sir Walter Scott chose to name Jarlshof for his novel *The Pirate*. That house was all that was visible until severe storms at the end of the 19th century tore off layers of turf and sand from dwellings that had been there since 2500 BC. The site was continuously inhabited for 4,000 years. Excavated remains include the house of a bronze smith (800 BC), a later Iron Age *broch* tower, Pictish wheelhouses and Norse longhouses (9th century AD). The two lairds' houses of the 16th and 17th century, also in ruin, were built by Earl Robert Stewart and his son Patrick.

Fair Isle

The population of about 70 relies on tourism associated with the Bird Observatory founded there in 1948, and with the knitting of the traditional fairisle patterned jerseys, probably developed from early Nordic designs. Shipwrecks were commonplace until the two lighthouses were built on the island by Stevenson in 1892.

111

Cultural Notes

Bagpipes

People cannot decide whether the bagpipes are a military weapon designed to scare the enemy or a lilting musical instrument to bring a tear to the eye of the nostalgic Scottish patriot. In a sports stadium they are clearly both. Instrument or weapon, its music emerges from a windbag originally made out of a sheep's bladder, the tune is played on the finger holes of a melody pipe or *chanter* while the *drone* pipes sound a continuous single note. Bagpipes appeared in the Highlands as the *pibroch* in the 15th century, festive or pastoral in peacetime, then stirring the soldiers into battle or lamenting the fallen in defeat.

Edinburgh Festival

The world's biggest celebration of the arts—theatre, opera, dance, music, cinema, books, cabaret, stand-up comedy, even the gloriously kitschy Military Tattoo at Edinburgh Castle—started in 1947. Now, every year from the end of July to the end of August, thousands of visitors pour into the city to attend a wonderful mixture of establishment high-quality culture and a vast so-called "fringe" of irreverent, avant-garde, outrageous, sometimes obscene, sometimes brilliant, often silly, events. The exhilarating atmosphere belies the city's reputation for being overly solemn and dignified. It is fun, serious fun. The main Festival has its headquarters and ticket-office at The Hub on Castlehill, publishing its programme in April, www.edinburghfestivals.co.uk.

Venues are scattered across the city in theatres, concert halls, clubs, pubs, churches, hotels and tents set up in public squares. The Fringe has outgrown the official Festival and now numbers nearly 1,000 events, programme from June at www.edfringe.com.

Glasgow School

Coming to prominence in the 1880s, the Glasgow School took a straightforward and unsentimental approach to its painting that broke with Scotland's romantic tradition. In their landscapes, Robert Macaulay Stevenson, William York Macgregor, John Lavery and Edward Hornel distrusted the mountain and moorland scenes painted for Victorian mansions. Inspired by French painters of the Barbizon school and later the Impressionists, they were the first Scottish artists committed to painting in the open air, with more vigorous results than were achieved by predecessors sketching romantic backdrops to be finished back in the studio. The talented Bessie MacNicol proved that the school's combination of stylistic ruggedness and decorative harmony was for woman as well as men.

Mercat Cross

The Mercat or Market Cross originally symbolized a burgh's right to engage in trade. Documents suggest the first crosses stood on the market place in the 12th century and were made of wood. Many of the sandstone crosses seen today date back to the 16th and 17th centuries, while others, more elaborately carved, were erected in the Victorian era. Bigger towns like Aberdeen had more than one—a Fish Cross and Meat Cross—according to what was sold at the market. Most crosses are crowned with a heraldic or religious emblem other than an actual cross.

Charles Rennie Mackintosh

The Glasgow-born architect and designer (1868–1928) carved out a unique place for himself in European art with buildings and furniture that unified the crisp rectangular lines of the Industrial Age with the delicate languid curves of Art Nouveau. After studying at the Glasgow School of Art, he incorporated his taste for the functional and decorative in his design for the school's new building. With his wife, Margaret Macdonald, he worked in metal, glass, enamel and lacquered wood to design furniture and interiors for Glasgow tea-rooms with a lack of ornate excess that had a great influence on Viennese architects and designers. His erratic temperament, however, alienated clients and in 1913 he turned from architecture to painting still-lifes and landscapes.

Tartan

The cloth of cross-checked patterns has become a pillar of the Scottish tourist industry. The Scottish Tartans Society founded in 1963 keeps a "Register of All Known Tartans", currently about 1,300 and growing, for anyone with a real or imagined connection to a Scottish clan. A heavy woollen, practically rainproof, tartan cape was first known to be worn by Highlanders in the 16th century but did not become common until the late 17th and 18th century. Adapted for kilts and other clothes, a bright pattern was worn for ceremonies and battles, while a plain, duller pattern served for everyday wear. After the Jacobite rebellion of 1745, tartans were banned until Highland regiments started wearing them again in the 1780s, each with its own design. With the state visit of George IV to Edinburgh in 1822, military fashion launched the fad for civilian clans to claim their own pattern.

Sports

Many come to Scotland just for its sporting facilities, perhaps because the outdoor sports enable them to enjoy sightseeing at the same time in the country's glorious landscapes.

Golf

The birthplace of golf offers visitors more than 400 courses all over the country on which to test their skills, most often in beautiful surroundings flanked by woodlands and the sea shore. It is from the latter that golf links take their name, from the medieval *hlinc*, coastal sandy-soil grassland or dune, where the original courses and bunkers were laid out. In Scotland all golf courses are open to the public. For more experienced golfers, even the most prestigious championship courses like St Andrews, Carnoustie, Royal Troon or Gleaneagles are accessible to anyone with a handicap certificate (24 for men, 36 for women) though they usually have to book two or three months in advance. (St Andrews, which now has five courses, also organizes a daily right-to-play lottery for people entering their name before 2pm on the day they want to play.) The Scottish Tourist Board can advise about a regional "golf pass".

Fishing

Despite the quality and abundance of salmon, pike, perch and trout (brown, rainbow and sea), fishing in Scotland remains a solitary and uncrowded sport. Anglers enjoy the huge variety of the country's waterways—the Tay, Tweed, Dee and Spey rivers and fast-flowing mountain streams, vast expanses of lochs and the indented coastlines around the mainland and islands. No fishing licence is needed, just a regional permit, usually available through the local tackle-shop or fishing club (details from the tourist office). Coarse fishing and sea angling have no close season, while regional tourist offices will advise about local seasonal restrictions on trout and salmon fishing. Deepsea fishing in the north can catch you dogfish, halibut, mackerel and skate.

Swimming and Water Sports

The best and cleanest sandy beaches and coves are out on the islands, although the beaches of

Wester Ross and Caithness come close, but even there, only the hardiest of swimmers are tempted by the cool, cool waters. Hardiest of all are the surfers who brave the breakers up on the north coast at Thurso or the Atlantic coasts of the island of Islay. Sailing, wind-surfing and canoeing are popular on the lochs and the islands, with especially good facilities at Balloch on Loch Lomond, Lamlash on Arran and Portree on Skye.

Hiking and Biking

The Lowlands and Highlands are made for walkers and cyclists. Three great Long Distance Footpaths—Southern Uplands Way from coast to coast, West Highlands Way from Glasgow to Fort William and Speyside Way through malt whisky country—are clearly mapped for walkers to take whatever short section they choose. Rangers of the National Trust for Scotland provide guided walks through the woodlands at Glencoe and from Torridon around the loch. Other popular hill walking areas are the Cuillins on Skye and west of Loch Ness along Glen Shiel and Kintail Ridge. Tourist offices provide maps for forest cycle-trails

Pony Trekking, Horse Riding

Pony trekking along beaches, clifftop trails or across rolling moorland is one of the more delightful Scottish contributions to western civilization. Riding centres and trails all over the country have received the seal of approval of the Trekking and Riding Society of Scotland—details from the Scottish Tourist Board. The same centres also provide horses for more experienced and energetic riders.

Rugby Union

Scotland's home games in the Six Nations tournament against England, Wales, Ireland, France and Italy are played at Murrayfield Stadium in Edinburgh. Club rugby is concentrated in the south of the country. The fast-moving seven-a-side version is played in the Borders, the Melrose Sevens Week taking place in April.

Football

To the outsider, Scottish club football means Glasgow Celtic and Glasgow Rangers, known collectively as the Old Firm—the only teams to make a regular impact on the European scene. Their fierce rivalry is heightened by a traditional religious identification—Catholic Celtic and Protestant Rangers—and many Glasgow pubs display notices warning customers "No Football Shirts Allowed". Celtic play at Parkhead, Rangers at Ibrox Stadium, while international games are played at Hampden Park.

Shopping

In an era of increasing worldwide conformity, Scotland still offers a wide range of items that are distinctly Scottish. Only local water and know-how make real Scotch. And no one ever invented a tackier souvenir than a toy Loch Ness monster.

Where?

The main cities—Edinburgh, Glasgow and Inverness—are the obvious places to find the largest selection of items, even from the remoter parts of Scotland. Even the prices are not so very different, though you may find it more fun buying malt whisky from its distillery on the Whisky Trail or a sweater in a shop just down the road from the herd of Shetland sheep providing the raw material. In Edinburgh, Princes Street has the big chain stores, Cockburn Street is more chic, while Grassmarket, Canongate and Lawnmarket are good for woollen goods. In Glasgow, Princes Square is the place to go, as well as Buchanan and Sauchiehall Streets and St Enoch Shopping Centre. In Inverness, High Street's pedestrian zone is the city's shopping hub.

Food

The infamous haggis may be the most uniquely Scottish of gourmet specialities, but there are many other tasty souvenirs to take home: smoked salmon, marmalade (especially whisky-flavoured), crumbly shortbread, oat cakes, Orkney fudge and butterscotch (also known as the dentist's delight).

Jewellery and Glassware

Distinctive Scottish silver and gold jewellery uses Celtic emblems, while you will find old Norse patterns in Orkney and Shetland silverware. Edinburgh Crystal, Scotland's only hand-made glass manufacturer, produces splendid wine goblets and other glassware at Penicuik, a half-hour drive south of Edinburgh.

Knitwear

Shetland sweaters, plain or with brightly coloured fairisle patterns, cashmeres, scarves, throws, rugs: the variety of woollens is enormous, the workmanship of highest quality.

Tartan is now made in many beautiful colour combinations.

Tartans

Tartan kilts and waistcoats can be seen worn at all levels of Scottish society. De rigueur for Highland family weddings as well as for smart city balls for the monied classes, the kilt is also worn with pride by Scottish rugby and football fans. Some of the more dignified shops will check your family name in their computer to let you know which clan tartan you are entitled to wear (but this is not on historic grounds: up until the 19th century, no attempt was made to match a pattern exclusively to any one clan). Ties, dolls, underwear, bikinis and bagpipes—anything goes.

Tweeds

From the island of Lewis and Harris, the rough Harris tweed, coloured by natural dyes from plants and lichen, is perfect for a sturdy country jacket, skirt or suit. Softer, more expensive, tweeds may be mixed with cashmere.

Whisky

If you want to buy your single malt at source, the island of Islay, Lochranza on Arran, Campbeltown on Kintyre or the Highland distilleries on Speyside are the places to stop. Many come in fancy tall cartons or tins that make excellent pasta containers. 117

Dining Out

It is the sheer high quality of Scottish produce that makes good eating here such a delightful surprise. And well-entrenched immigrant communities in the big towns add some colourful and first-rate Italian, Indian and Chinese alternatives.

Breakfast

If you have a real Scottish breakfast, you won't need much lunch. A good B&B will feed you for the day—oatmeal porridge (which Scots eat with salt rather than sugar, but you're not obliged to follow suit), then besides the usual English bacon, sausage and eggs, a choice of Arbroath smokies (smoked haddock), kippers, black pudding and potato scones. Or the whole lot! Unless you specify otherwise, tea will usually be served strong and coffee weak. Bread rolls should come hot, with terrific jams and marmalades, often home made.

Soups

The Scots tackle their climate with a great variety of hearty soups. Two vie for the title of the national soup: Scotch broth (barley, lentils, mutton or beef and vegetables) and the startling cock-a-leekie, combining chicken, leeks, diced ham and prunes. Partan bree is a cream of crab soup, Cullen skink a creamy soup of smoked haddock with onions and potatoes. Oatmeal soup, porridge upgraded to dinner, is creamed with onion, leek and other vegetables.

Fish

Salmon, farmed or, more subtly-flavoured, wild from the rivers Tweed, Tay or Spey, is served smoked as a starter or hot with vegetables. Brown, rainbow or sea trout make excellent alternatives. Herrings are popular, often soused in vinegar, or coated in oatmeal and fried. On the coast, shellfish includes crab, scallops, prawns, mussels and oysters.

Meat

Aberdeen Angus beef is as good as any in Europe. Lamb and high quality mutton are popular on the islands. Venison is served as a stew or roasted. The choicest game birds are the succulent and tangy grouse and the milder pheasant, the latter often with a spicy stuffing of oatmeal and onion. Sauces to accompany these meats are often very Scottish in flavour, using whisky and the hedgerow fruits which grow so well, such as brambles, rowanberries and raspberries.

Dessert
The Scots prefer to say pudding, best of all Cranachan, another oatmeal concoction toasted and variously doused in rum or whisky, with fresh raspberries or strawberries and whipped cream. Atholl Brose mixes honey-sweetened oatmeal with whisky and cream. Tarts of ginger or rhubarb are also popular.

Drinks
Stronger, smoother and heavier than most of its English counterparts, thick dark Scottish beer is served by the pint or half-pint, not icy cold but room temperature, with a full head of foam to prove it did not come flat out of the tap. While most beers on offer come from big-name breweries, connoisseurs recommend looking out for the small local breweries to be found throughout Scotland.

Whisky—*uisge beatha*, "water of life"—is of course the national drink. More than 90% is sold in its blended form, seven parts grain whisky, three parts single malt. These may be drunk in a shot glass as a "chaser" to a pint of beer or in ice as a long drink. The finer single malt whiskies are best drunk neat, to appreciate the distinctive flavour.

HAGGIS
According to the Oxford English Dictionary, gourmet efforts to assimilate the supreme Scottish delicacy etymologically to the French *hachis* (mince) has "no basis of fact". No, haggis ("Derivation unknown") is Scottish through and through and nothing to be scared of. This savoury pouch of sheep's stomach is stuffed with chopped liver, heart and other innards, oatmeal, onions, spices and suet, and boiled to be served with *chappit tatties* and *bashed neeps*—mashes of potatoes and turnips. Wonderful. As Robert Burns, in whose honour the dish is consumed by the thousand all over the Scottish world on his birthday, January 25, so aptly said in his *Address to a Haggis*:
"Ye Pow'rs, wha mak mankind your care,
And dish them out their bill o' fare,
Auld Scotland wants nae skinking ware
That jaups in luggies;
But, if ye wish her gratefu' prayer
Gie her a haggis!"

119

The Hard Facts

Airports

Scotland's main airport is Glasgow. It is about 20 minutes from the city centre and 2 minutes from Paisley, the nearest town. Taxi and bus services (running every 10–15 minutes during the day, every 30 minutes in the evening) are available. International and domestic flights also serve Prestwick, Edinburgh, Aberdeen, Inverness and Shetland (Sumburgh). The terminals all provide banking, car-hire and tourist information services, in addition to duty-free shop, restaurant and snack bar facilities.

Climate

Erratic is the best description. The Atlantic brings in the rain and winds, but the Gulf Stream tempers the climate. The west coast is wetter but warmer than the east coast. May and June are the best months, most sunshine and relatively little rain. July and August are the warmest months, average daily maximum temperatures around 18°C (65°F) in Edinburgh, but midges become a problem in the north. September and October can be delightfully sunny, but the rain sets in, too. Warm waterproof clothing and an umbrella are a year-round must.

Communications

Apart from taking care of your mail, the post offices offer other services such as money exchange, telephone, fax and internet connection, and sell fishing licences (www.postoffice.co.uk). The sub post-offices in small towns and villages are often combined with newsagents and grocery stores.

If you have urgent mail, ask your hotel about the international courier services available. Hotels usually let you use their fax service. Much cheaper than hotel room-phones, public payphones accept British coins and most accept credit cards and pre-paid phone cards, available at newsagents and post offices. Mobile phones can be rented in the larger cities. Public Internet centres are springing up all over the country, both in cafés and local libraries.

Crime

Away from some "problem" neighbourhoods in the big cities, Scotland is as safe as anywhere on earth. As anywhere these days, pickpockets do work the major tourist centres. Without being paranoid, you will avoid trouble with elementary precautions. Leave your valuables in the hotel safe and keep your belongings out of sight when parking your car. Keep photocopies of your passport, driver's license, travel tickets and credit cards separate from the originals, or scan them and send them to yourself as an e-mail attachment so you can access them in case of need.

Driving

If you intend to rent a car, be sure to have a valid national licence or International Driving Permit. Payment is almost always by credit card only. Check on the exact extent of insurance coverage, personal, fire, collision, theft, etc. Roads, except in the remotest mountain areas, are excellent. As in England, drive on the left, overtake on the right. Unless otherwise posted, maximum speed on motorways and dual carriageways is 70 mph (110 kph), on most other roads 60 mph (100 kph), in built-up areas 30 or 40 mph (50 or 65 kph). Out in the country, there are many single-track roads and lots of sheep. The use of seatbelts is compulsory, front and rear.

Electric Current

Britain's electric current is 240 volts AC, 50 cycles. Continental European visitors will need an adaptor for the three-point plugs. North American appliances need a transformer and adaptor.

Emergencies

Most problems can be handled at your hotel desk. The emergency telephone number for police, fire, ambulance or coastguard is 999. Consular help is there only for critical situations, lost passports or worse, not for lost cash or plane tickets.

Essentials

Travel light, especially as far as clothing is concerned. Unless you enjoy dressing up for the theatre or smart restaurants, you won't need much formal wear. Pack a sun-hat for summer but warm waterproof clothing and an umbrella are a year-round must. Good walking shoes are vital, especially for the mountains. Bring along sun-block, insect-repellent and a pocket torch in case of (rare) electricity cuts.

Formalities

A valid passport is all that non-British citizens will need. In these days of heightened immigration controls, you may be asked on entry to show your return ticket. No special health certificates are required for European or North American citizens.

Health

Most holiday health problems are from too much sun—even in Scotland. Avoid excessive direct exposure to the summer sun,

121

especially at the seaside. Wear a hat and use a sun-screen. Insect bites from midges and other insects can be a bother in summer, so bring plenty of insect-repellent. Hospital care is good, but medical fees can be expensive if you do not have proper health insurance. Holders of a European Health Card are entitled to free medical treatment at National Health Service hospitals. Some non-EU countries like Australia and New Zealand have reciprocal arrangements. Check before leaving home. If you anticipate need of prescription medicines, take your own as you may not find the exact equivalent on the spot.

Language
English is of course the local language, even in the Highland and the islands where some Gaelic is spoken.

Media
The main British newspapers, serious broadsheet and lighter tabloid, are all available, but the Scottish papers are well worth a look to get the local view and programmes of local events: *The Scotsman* in Edinburgh, *The Herald* of Glasgow, *Press and Journal* of Aberdeen and the *Dundee Courier*. Scotland's own tabloid and best-selling paper is the *Daily Record*. TV is served by the BBC and three independent channels,

in addition to the numerous cable channels available in some hotels. The excellent BBC Radio Scotland provides the best Scottish view of politics, arts and sport.

Money
On the whole more Europhile than England, Scotland is nonetheless bound to Sterling currency, albeit using Scottish banknotes, legal tender throughout Britain (£100, £50, £20, £10, £5 and £1). Coins are issued for £2, £1, 50 pence, 20p, 10p, 5p, 2p and 1p. International credit cards are accepted. ATM cashpoint machines are plentiful, almost wherever you see a bank or building society.

Opening Hours
We give the following times as a general guide, some of them subject to variations.
Banks: Monday to Friday 9 or 9.30 a.m. to 4 or 5 p.m., some slightly later on Thursday.
Shops: in the bigger towns, opening hours have extended dramatically from the traditional 9 a.m. to 5.30 or 6 p.m. Many shopping centres and supermarkets now stay open Monday to Saturday to 8 or 9 p.m., even for six hours on Sunday. Some of the larger supermarkets now boast 24-hour, 7-day opening. Shops in the Highlands and Islands usually close on Sunday, and small towns often

apply an early closing policy, usually Wednesday, at 1 p.m.

Post Offices: Monday to Friday 9 a.m.–5.30 p.m., Saturday 9 a.m.–12.30 p.m.

Museums and Monuments vary considerably from season to season and year to year. Check with local tourist information office.

Photography

If you are still using a standard camera, you'll find every imaginable form of film available, with super-fast development services. Most museums allow cameras, but sometimes for an extra fee, with restrictions on the use of flash.

Public Transport

Train. The railway network does not cover the whole country and is best used for the main towns—between Glasgow, Edinburgh, Stirling, Perth, Dundee and Aberdeen. However, the West Highland Railway's scenic routes offer a sightseeing experience in many places otherwise available only to hikers—from Glasgow to Fort William and Mallaig and from Inverness to Kyle of Lochalsh.

Bus. Slower but cheaper than the train, the largest network of intercity buses is operated by Scottish Citylink. Remote areas in the Highlands and Islands are served by the Royal Mail's postbuses.

For anybody not in a hurry, these minibuses take up to ten fare-paying passengers on postal delivery routes up hill and down dale. The Scottish Tourist Board provides routes and timetables, or see www.royalmail.com.

Ferry. Scotland's 60 inhabited islands, but also "short cuts" across mainland inlets, make the country's ferry services a vital part of public transportation. Most of the ferries carry vehicles, and drivers need to book a long time in advance to be sure of a berth. The main service from the west coast to the Inner and Outer Hebrides is operated by Caledonian MacBrayne (better known simply as CalMac). Northlink Ferries and John O'Groats Ferries run services to the Orkney and Shetland Islands.

Tipping

There is no general rule, but the custom is 10 to 15% for waiters, taxi-drivers, hairdressers and tour guides and 50p–£1 per day for staff in larger hotels. Bar staff in pubs do not expect tips but it's nice to buy them a drink occasionally.

Toilets

Public toilets in restaurants, cafés, museums and hotels are generally much cleaner than in pubs, train and bus stations. You may sometimes need to pay 10p or 20p.

ORKNEY

INDEX

127

INDEX

GENERAL EDITOR
  Barbara Ender-Jones
EDITOR
  Nicola Taylor
LAYOUT
  Luc Malherbe
PHOTO CREDITS
  K. Ohlhoff: inside front cover
  laif/Krinitz: pp. 1, 2, 4, 7, 37,
    58, 68, 73, 76, 85, 93, 117
  –/Zielke H&D: p. 16
  Hémisphères/Frilet: p. 13
  –/Rieger: pp. 23, 27, 33, 78,
    97, 102, 107
  –/Wysocki: pp. 30, 45, 63
  –/Boisberranger: p. 111
  Look/Pompe: pp. 88, 100
  Corbis/Niall Benvie: p. 48
  –/Vittoriano Rastelli: p. 57
  –/Franz-Marc Frei: p. 82
MAPS
  Elsner & Schichor
  JPM Publications

Printed in Switzerland
Weber/Bienne (CTP) — 05/12/01
Edition 2006

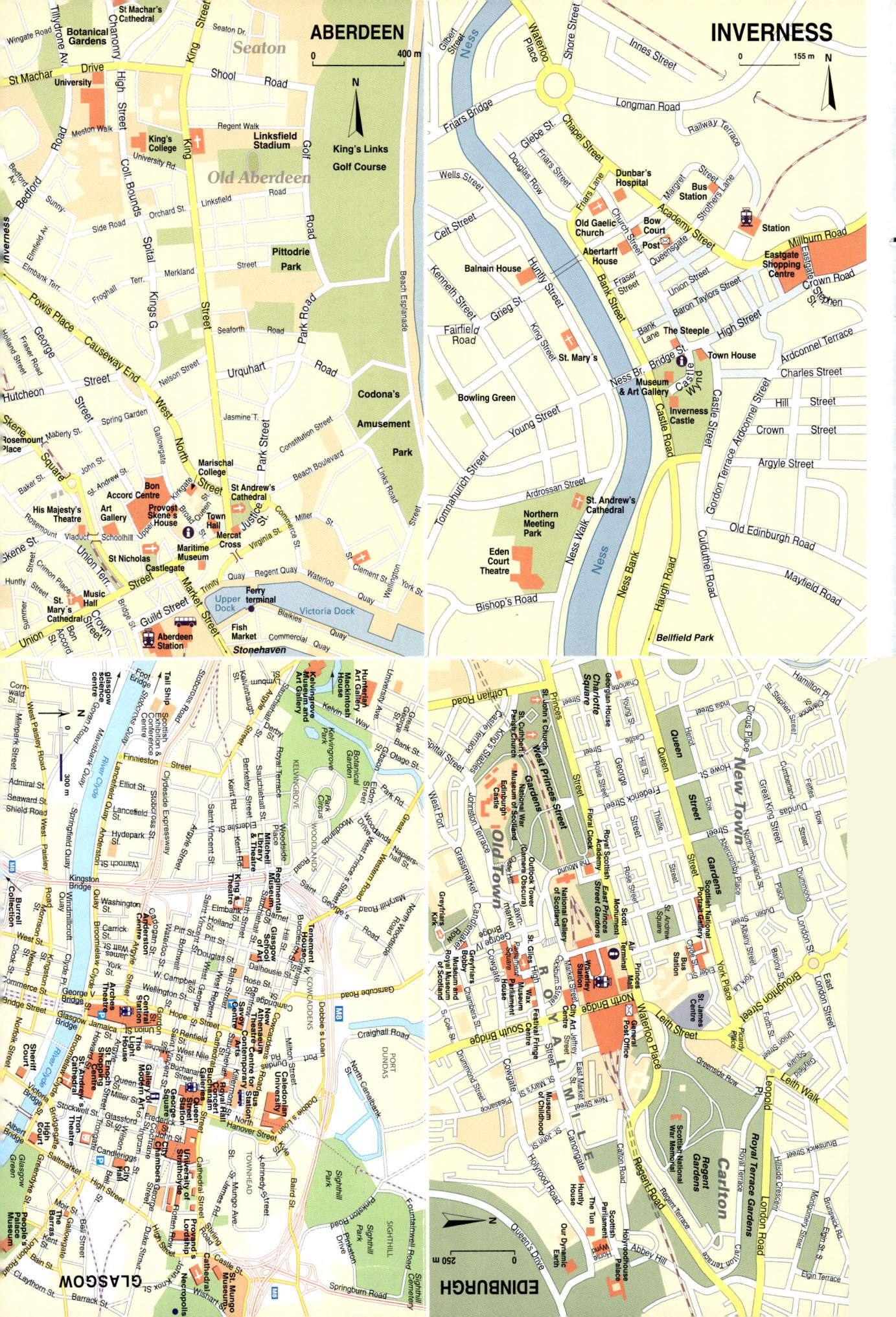

SCOTLAND

0   50 km

N

Atlantic Ocean

North Sea

Inset map
SCOTLAND
Edinburgh
NORTHERN IRELAND
Belfast
IRELAND
Dublin
Irish Sea
ENGLAND
WALES
Cardiff
London
English Channel
Atlantic Ocean
North Sea

Orkney / North
Hollandstoun
Westray   Rapness
Rousay Eday Sanday
Brinyan   Braeswick
Mainland Backa- Whitehall
Tingwall land Stronsay
Shapinsay
Stromness Kirkwall
Hoy   Orkney
South Ronaldsay
Burwick
John o'Groats
Duncansby Head

Mainland labels
Cape Wrath
Durness Melvich Thurso
Kinlochbervie Bettyhill Dunnet Head Scrabster
Handa Tongue CAITHNESS Wick
Scourie Ben Hope 927m
Oldany SUTHERLAND Latheron
Skiag Bridge Ben More Assynt 998m Loch Rimsdale Kinbrace
Lochinver Altnaharra
Ledmore Loch Shin Helmsdale
Achiltibuie Lairg Golspie Brora
Summer Isles HIGHLANDS Bonar Bridge Dunrobin Castle
Ullapool Dornoch Tarbat Ness
Ardgay Tain Portmahomack

Butt of Lewis
Port of Ness
Barvas
Flannan Is.
Carloway Stornoway
Isle of Lewis
Brenish Balallan
Hushinish
Taransay Tarbert Shiant Is.
Harris Scalpay Rubha Reidh
Pabbay Leverburgh
Bernaray Rodel
Tigharry Newtonferry Rubha Hunish
Monach Is. North Uist Taffin
Uachdar Lochmaddy Uig Rona
Creagorry Isle of Skye
Dunvegan Portree Raasay
South Uist Bracadale
Carbost Applecross
Daliburg Cuillin Hills Kyle of Lochalsh
Lochboisdale Broadford Dornie
Eriskay Elgol Eilean Donan Castle Shiel Bridge
Barra Kyleakin
Barraigh
Canna Rhum
Kinloch Armadale Loch Quoich
Eigg Mallaig Invergarry
Airsaig Loch Morar Loch Lochy
Muck Lochailort Glenfinnan
Acharacle Spean Bridge
Ardnamurchan Loch Shiel Fort William
Kilchoan Salen Strontian
Arinagour Morvern Ben Nevis 1343m
Tobermory Lochaline Castle Stalker
Coll Fishnish Loch Linnhe Glencoe
Isle of Mull Pier Craignure
Tiree Ben More 966m Lismore Dunstaffnage Castle
Scarinish Ulva Lochdon Oban Taynuilt
Staffa Fionnphort Dalmally
Iona Abbey Iona Firth of Lorn
Scarba Crianlarich
Colonsay Inveraray Loch Katrine
Scalasaig Ford Arrochar Callander
Ardlussa Lochgilphead Aberfoyle Dunblane
Jura Hill House Luss Stirling
Islay Kilberry Stones Helensburgh Loch Lomond
Port Askaig Loch Fyne Dunoon Alexandria Antonine Wall
Portnahaven Kames Gourock Dumbarton Wall
Rinns Point Tarbert Bute Port Glasgow Kilsyth Linlithgow
Bridgend Rothesay Greenock Cumbernauld Falkirk
Bowmore Johnstone Paisley Coatbridge Airdrie Livingston
Port Ellen Largs GLASGOW Motherwell Whitburn
Gigha Dalry Hamilton Larkhall
Ardbeg Clachan Stewarton East Kilbride Lanark
Glenbarr Lochranza Ardrossan Kilmarnock Lesmahagow
Kintyre Brodick Castle Irvine Galston Biggar
Campbeltown Arran Troon Dundonald Castle Peebles
Machrihanish Holy Island Prestwick Mauchline Crawford
Rathlin Ayr Auchinleck Cumnock
Mull of Kintyre Southend Culzean Castle Maybole New Cumnock
Bushmills Turnberry Dalmellington Moffat
Ballycastle Girvan AYRSHIRE Drumlanrig Castle
Armoy Ballantrae Merrick 843m Thornhill Hermitage Castle
Glenariff Milleur Point New Galloway Langholm
NORTHERN IRELAND Castle Kennedy Gardens Newton Stewart DUMFRIES & GALLOWAY Lockerbie
Ballymena North Channel Stranraer Castle Douglas Dumfries Annan Gretna green
Larne Portpatrick Wigtown Dalbeattie Caerlaverock Castle
Island Magee Glenluce Kirkcudbright Solway Firth Carlisle
Antrim Luce Bay Logan Botanic Gardens Port William Silloth
Newtownabbey Drummore Wigtown Bay Wigton
Bangor Isle of Whithorn Maryport Aspatria Penrith
Belfast Newtownards Mull of Galloway Workington Cockermouth
Lisburn Strangford Lough Whitehaven Keswick
Lurgan Saintfield Portaferry Point of Ayre Lake District National Park Brough
Ballynahinch Downpatrick Bride Egremont Ambleside Windermere Kendal
Isle of Man Seascale CUMBRIA Kirkby Stephen
Ramsey Ravenglass Yorkshire Dales National Park

Invergordon Alness Cromarty Moray Firth Burghead Branderburgh Portknockie Macduff Fraserburgh
Strathpeffer Ding-wall Fort-rose Nairn Elgin Fochabers Cullen Banff New Deer Peterhead
Muir of Ord Fort George Forres Glen Grant Distillery Keith Strathisla Distillery Turriff Deigatie Castle Mintlaw
Black Isle Cawdor Castle MORAY Dufftown Rhynie Huntly Fyvie Castle Ellon Oldmeldrum
Inverness Glenfiddich Distillery Leith Hall Inverurie Dyce
Drumna-drochit Grantown-on-Spey Glenlivet Distillery ABERDEEN-SHIRE Aberdeen
Loch Ness Cannich Tomintoul Cairngorms National Nature Reserve Craigievar Castle Drum Castle
Loch Ness Monster Centre Carn Eige 1183m Aviemore Cairn Gorm 1245m Cairn Gorm Mts. Aboyne Crathes Castle
Fort Augustus Kincraig Ben Macdui 1309m Balmoral Castle Crathie Banchory
Monadhliath Mountains Kingussie Royal Lochnagar Distillery Stonehaven
Glen Albyn Newtonmore Braemar Grampian Dunnottar Castle
Loch Lochy Laggan Dalwhinnie Inverbervie
Glen More Loch Laggan Clova Edzell
Loch Ericht Blair Castle House of Dun Brechin
Schiehallion 1083m Pitlochry Kirriemuir Montrose
Loch Rannoch Aberfeldy ANGUS Forfar Lunan
Dunkeld Blairgowrie Glamis Castle Arbroath
PERTHSHIRE Loch Tay Crieff Perth Carnoustie
Lochearnhead Newport-on-Tay Monifieth Dundee
STIRLING Kinross Earlshall Castle North Sea
Tillicoultry Alloa Cowden-beath Glenrothes Cupar St. Andrews
Culross Kirkcaldy FIFE Crail Fife Ness
Bo'ness Dunfermline Buckhaven Anstruther
Grangemouth Firth of Forth Isle of May
Bo'ness North Berwick Tantallon Castle
EDINBURGH Musselburgh Dunbar Cockburnspath
Dalkeith Haddington St. Abbs Eyemouth
Penicuik Gorebridge LOTHIAN Lauder Duns Berwick-upon-Tweed
Moorfoot Hills Lammermuir Hills Coldstream Manderstone House
BORDERS Galashiels Kelso Holy Island Lindisfarne
Traquair House Melrose Selkirk Dryburgh Abbey Belford
Hawick Jedburgh Northumberland Wooler
The Cheviot Hills NORTHUMBERLAND Alnwick
Newbiggin-by-the-Sea
National Park Morpeth Blyth
ENGLAND Blaydon Whitley Bay Tynemouth
Hadrian's Wall Hexham Whickham Newcastle Upon-Tyne Gateshead
Caerlaverock Castle Brampton Stanley Consett Chester-le-Street Sunderland
Carlisle Alston St. John's Chapel Stanhope Bishop Auckland Durham Peterlee
Wigton Barnard Castle Stockton-Middlesbrough-on-Tees Hartlepool
Wordsworth House Penrith Appleby Darlington Great Ayton North York Moors National Park
Keswick Barnard Castle Richmond Guisborough
Kirby Stephen Northallerton